IT IS THE LORD

IT IS THE LORD

by

MARCUS L. LOANE, M.A., D.D.
Bishop Coadjutor in the Diocese of Sydney

Foreword by

L. L. MORRIS, B.D., M.Th., B.Sc., Ph.D.
Principal, Ridley College, Melbourne

London
MARSHALL, MORGAN AND SCOTT
Edinburgh

LONDON

MARSHALL, MORGAN AND SCOTT, LTD.
1–5 PORTPOOL LANE
HOLBORN, E.C.1

AUSTRALIA AND NEW ZEALAND

117–119 BURWOOD ROAD
MELBOURNE E.13

SOUTH AFRICA

P.O. BOX 1720, STURK'S BUILDINGS
CAPE TOWN

CANADA

EVANGELICAL PUBLISHERS
241 YONGE STREET
TORONTO

Made and Printed in Great Britain by C. Tinling & Co. Ltd.,
Liverpool, London and Prescot.

To
PETER and VERA
"True yoke-fellows . . . in the Gospel"

"Lift up thy face unto God . . . and light shall shine
upon thy ways."   —JOB 22: 26.28

"If Christ be not risen," wrote St. Paul, "then is our preaching vain, and your faith is also vain" (1 Cor. 15: 14). So he brought out the fact that the Resurrection of our Lord is of critical importance to Christians. This is not some minor episode, not an incident which may casually be jettisoned without affecting the faith in any significant manner. It is at the very heart of Christianity. If it is not true, then the whole faith, in the great Apostle's words, is "vain".

It is for this reason that Christians come back to the Cross and the Resurrection again and again. It is not a coincidence that the great Christian festival is Easter, that time of the year when we commemorate our Lord's victory over death and hell and every force of evil. Those who are the Lord's delight to dwell on the wonder of this great truth.

That is why we must be grateful to Bishop Loane for his book. Here we are taken step by step through the narratives of the resurrection appearances. Those who have read his previous books in this series on the Passion and the Resurrection will give this book an eager welcome. And they will not be disappointed. They will find here the same mastery of the subject, the same devout and reverent approach, the same careful attention to detail, the same wide knowledge of Scripture. Bishop Loane is a master of the art of writing devotional commentaries and this slim volume is up to his highest standard. There may be reason for doubt as to his interpretation of some disputed passages (I rather doubt one or two things myself!). But there is no room for doubting that this is a penetrating and deeply spiritual writing. No attentive reader can fail to be profited.

It is a privilege to have been asked to write a Foreword to it. I am very glad to commend it, for I know it will refresh the spirit of many.

LEON MORRIS
Ridley College
Melbourne

CONTENTS

THE RISEN SAVIOUR

We find ourselves in the presence of a great mystery when we try to contemplate the real nature of the risen body of the Lord Jesus. When He rose from the grave, He rose to die no more; He would never again be subject to the power of death, for "death hath no more dominion over Him" (Rom. 6: 9). His body was endowed with properties and qualities which were new and mysterious; it was totally different both in action and in being from the limitations which had prevailed "in the days of His flesh" (Heb. 5: 7). He could appear and vanish at will in a manner that was wholly spontaneous and supernormal; He could ignore or transcend natural barriers in a way that is quite beyond ordinary comprehension. Thus He emerged from the graveclothes while not a single fold was displaced (John 20: 5), and He left the tomb even though the stone had yet to be rolled away (Matt. 28: 2). He revealed Himself to Mary in the garden and then to the women by the wayside, and He withdrew again without a hint to tell them how He came or where He went (John 20: 14.17; Matt. 28: 9.10). He joined the two disciples on the way to Emmaus as though He had come from nowhere (Luke 24: 15), and He left them in the inn at the village as though He had vanished into space (Luke 24: 31). He was present at no great interval of time in two distinct places at some distance from each other, first with the Two in Emmaus (Luke 24: 31) and then with Simon Peter near Jerusalem (Luke 24: 34). Twice He stood in the midst of the disciples who had assembled behind shut doors and iron bolts, and there was no obvious means of ingress or egress (John 20: 19; 20: 26). His manifestations to the Seven by the Lake and to the brethren on the hills of Galilee were no less sudden and unexplained (John 21: 4; Matt. 28: 16). It would seem that all the Resurrection appearances were marked by this dramatic quality. No one knew where He was in the intervals between each appearance or whence He came on each occasion. Yet the Gospel records make it plain that His body risen was identical with His body buried. They all insist upon the reality and identity of the resurrection body under tests of sense to which He Himself appealed. There are two main lines of testimony which have a strong bearing on this question.

The first line of testimony points to the fact that this was A REAL BODY. Proof of this may be found in the series of manifestations to the disciples: "To whom also He showed Himself alive after His Passion by many infallible proofs, being seen of them forty days, and speaking of the things pertaining to the Kingdom of God" (Acts 1: 3). Ten such occasions have been placed on record, and their history leaves no doubt as to His resurrection reality. The first five took place on the very day when He rose again; the other five took place from time to time during the forty days that followed. He appeared to Mary in the garden and the women by the wayside in the early morning (John 20: 11.18; Matt. 28: 9.10). Then He appeared to the disciples on the way to Emmaus and to Simon Peter in the late afternoon (Luke 24: 13.32; 24: 34). Then He revealed Himself in the course of the same evening to the band of apostles and disciples in the room in Jerusalem (John 20: 19.23; Luke 24: 33.43). Eight days later, He appeared again to the disciples assembled in that room in order that Thomas might see and believe (John 20: 24.29). A lapse of time followed before He showed Himself to the Seven on the shore of Galilee (John 21: 1.14) and to some five hundred gathered on the hills above the sea (1 Cor. 15: 6; Matt. 28: 16.20). Then He was seen of James (1 Cor. 15: 7), and last of all by the men who watched Him ascend from the Mount of Olives (Luke 24: 50.53; Acts 1: 9.12). There may have been other occasions as well when He met the disciples in order to instruct them in the things of the Kingdom; but these ten are enough as proof of His resurrection reality. He was seen in private by ones and twos, and in public by many at once; He made Himself known by night and by day, both in Judaea and in Galilee. The same men saw Him more than once, and at times that were wide apart. They saw His face and heard His voice; and all that they saw and heard told them that the Lord in His risen body was real indeed.

And it was not as though they only saw Him with their eyes; they were also allowed to feel Him with their hands. It would seem that Mary fell at His feet and held them fast when she met Him in the garden; and it was this eager clasping of His limbs which called forth the gentle prohibition: "Touch Me not" (John 20: 17). She had felt Him, and found Him real; she had touched Him, and that was enough. Therefore He told

her to desist: "Do not continue to touch Me." When He
revealed Himself to the women shortly after this scene,
we are told that "they came, and held Him by the feet,
and worshipped Him" (Matt. 28: 9). They had not
been without fear and trepidation when they first heard
of the resurrection; that fear was not wholly allayed
even by the message of the angel or the sight of Jesus
Himself. It was only when they held Him by the feet
and felt Him with their hands that all their fears were
swallowed up in adoring certainty. So too it was when
He appeared to the disciples in the evening. They were
terrified by His sudden advent while the door was still
shut, and they were seized with dread less He were a
phantom or an apparition (Luke 24: 37; cf. Matt.
14 :26). But He at once took steps to dismiss their fears
and to convince them that He was real: "Handle Me,
and see", He said; "for a spirit hath not flesh and bones
as ye see Me have" (Luke 24: 39). A week later when
He appeared to them in the same room, He told Thomas
to put Him to the test of touch and sight: "Reach
hither thy finger, and behold My hands; and reach
hither thy hand, and thrust it into My side" (John
20: 27). Thus the reality of His risen body was tried
and proved by the normal means of sensory perception;
they saw Him with their eyes and they handled Him
with their hands in a way that told them that He was
real indeed (1 John 1: 1.2).

Another form of evidence is the fact that He eat with
them from time to time. The first occasion was when
the two disciples constrained Him to lodge with them
in Emmaus. He went in as a guest and sat down as a
host to sup with them and they with Him: "And it

came to pass as He sat at meat with them, He took bread, and blessed it, and brake, and gave to them" (Luke 24: 30). When He stood in the midst of the disciples that same evening, He dispelled their fears in the same way. He asked them if any food was available, and they gave Him a piece of broiled fish and some honeycomb: "And He took it, and did eat before them" (Luke 24: 43). Some time later He stood on the shore while the Seven were out on the waters of Galilee. When they had beached their boat and had drawn near, they found a fire of coals prepared with fish and bread to eat. They heard Him say: "Come and dine" (John 21: 12); then He took bread, and gave it to them, and fish likewise. St. Luke declares in the Preface to The Acts that "being assembled together with them, He charged them not to depart from Jerusalem, but to wait for the Promise of the Father" (Acts 1: 4 R.V.). A rare word is translated by the expression: "Being assembled together"; it could be rendered with equal accuracy as the margin suggests: "Eating with them". Thus it may well refer to a meal which He had eaten with them, and the reference to the Promise of the Father seems to link it with the occasion which is described in the Gospel: "And behold, I send the Promise of My Father upon you; but tarry ye in the City of Jerusalem until ye be endued with power from on high" (Luke 24: 49). Simon Peter was to recall such meals as proofs of His resurrection when he was called to the home of Cornelius: "Him God raised up the third day, and shewed Him openly . . . unto witnesses chosen before of God, even to us who did eat and drink with Him after He rose from the dead" (Acts 10: 40.41). Such facts provide

cumulative proof as to the reality of His resurrection
and throw some light on the nature of His risen body.
It was not subject to want and infirmity as it had been
before His death, yet it retained all the essential properties of a body. It occupied space, and it had a
definite form; it could be seen and touched, and He
could partake of a meal. There was much that would
be mysterious, and yet there was more than enough to
prove that He was real.

The next line of testimony points to the fact that this
was THE SAME BODY. Proof of this may be found in the
permanence of the stigmata which He bore in His
hands and feet and side. On that Easter evening when
He came and stood in the midst of those whom He had
loved, they heard Him say: "Peace be unto you"
(John 20: 19). Then without more ado, we read:
"When He had so said, He shewed unto them His
hands and His side" (John 20: 20). Why did He show
them the print of the nails and the mark of the spear?
Why did He fix their thoughts at once on the scars of
the Cross? It was His first action after that brief word
of greeting, and it must have held some special significance. It was only three days since the disciples had
last seen Him; they had all left Him and fled at the
hour of His arrest. Since then, He had been through a
whole world of pain and trouble; He had passed
through nameless sorrows in the darkness, thirst, and
death of the Cross. Would that terrible agony leave no
imprint on His visible appearance? His face may have
been scored with pain before; now the furrows of grief
and the lines of sorrow would be still more deeply

engraved: "His visage was so marred more than any
man, and His form more than the sons of men" (Isa.
52: 14). It was not as though He had passed through
pain alone, for He had gone through death as well; and
His outward aspect might have been so changed that
some would hardly know Him. Was it so strange that
the disciples were startled when He stood in their
midst? But when He shewed unto them His hands and
His side, it was enough. They saw the scars of the Cross
and they knew that it was He. Those marks were the
infallible proof that His body risen was identical with
His body buried.

St. Luke makes it clear that at first they were fright-
ened as well as startled; and their dismay was not only
because they were faced with One Who had passed
through the gates of sorrow and death. He stood before
them as a man, but they knew not how or whence He
had come. He was possessed of no ordinary body, for
He had put on the immortal splendour and the un-
fading beauty of the Resurrection. Three of them had
seen Him in the glory of His Transfiguration, and that
had been enough to show how His mortal body could
pass from one state to another without loss of identity.
But the others had not known Him except as the Man
of sorrows, and there may have been a majesty in His
appearance now of which they had no previous conception. It seems that there was a certain undefined
difference which was enough in some cases to delay or
prevent recognition. Mary knew not that it was Jesus,
but thought that He was the keeper of the garden (John
20: 14.15). He appeared "in another form" to the two
disciples on the road from Jerusalem (Mark 16: 12),

B

and "their eyes were holden that they should not know
Him" (Luke 24: 16). The Seven knew not that it was
Jesus Who stood on the shore of Galilee, but thought
that He was a stranger (John 21: 4). No doubt there
were other causes which would hinder recognition, but
they do not remove the hint that there may have been
some change in outward mien and aspect. This would
help to explain the fear of the disciples on His appearance; it would partly explain why they thought in terms
of some strange ghostly apparition. But He soothed their
fears with the words: "Behold My hands and My feet,
that it is I Myself: handle Me and see, for a spirit hath
not flesh and bones as ye see me have" (Luke 24: 39).
Then He held out His nail-pierced palms and laid bare
His spear-torn side: "And when He had thus spoken,
He shewed them His hands and His feet (Luke 24: 40).
It was as they beheld the print of the nails and the scar
of the spear that their fears subsided for ever. These
marks were the infallible proof that the One Who stood
before them was that same Person Who had died on the
Cross and been placed in the tomb.

One of the Twelve had been away when He appeared
that night, and he alone failed to share in the joy of
their discovery. He soon heard from his friends how they
had seen the Lord, but he met them with the same
unbelief with which they had met the women (cf. Luke
24: 11). He would not take their word, and vowed that
he would not believe unless the same proofs were offered
to him: "Except I shall see in His hands the print of the
nails and put my finger into the print of the nails, and
thrust my hand into His side, I will not believe" (John
20: 25). Eight days elapsed, and then Jesus stood once

more in the midst. He met Thomas with words which showed how well He knew his heart: "Reach hither thy finger, and behold My hands; and reach hither thy hand, and thrust it into My side: and be not faithless, but believing" (John 20: 27). The sound of that voice and the sight of those scars were enough; Thomas did not need to reach out his hand to touch and feel those limbs. He fell down at His feet with the cry of worship: "My Lord and my God" (John 20: 28). It was remarkable that His voice should have come through the experience of death unchanged, and its accent alone had been enough to make Him known in the case of Mary (John 20: 16). It was perhaps yet more remarkable that the marks of the Cross should still appear in His body when He rose from the grave, but no stronger facts could ever have been offered in proof of His identity. They were indelible testimony to the effect that His body was real and that it was the same.

Forty days were to pass after He burst the bands of death and rose again; then came the last scene of all with His Ascension from Olivet. He led the disciples as far as Bethany on the southern slopes of Olivet; there He gathered them round Him in farewell. The hands which had been nailed to the Cross were lifted up in blessing, and they saw once more those scars which were the seals of His atonement. Then while His hands were still upraised, He began to ascend: "And it came to pass while He blessed them, He was parted from them and carried up into heaven" (Luke 24: 51). On all other occasions, He had vanished with a suddenness which had left them breathless; but now He was

"parted from them" in a slow and deliberate movement
while they followed Him with their eyes. There was
wonderful delicacy in this as an unspoken illustration of
love; it would suggest that He held back from the final
human wrench as long as He could. Thus they saw Him
ascend in His risen body until a cloud received Him out
of sight (Acts 1: 9). He had gone up to take His place
at the right hand of God, but the angels told the wondering disciples that He will come again: "This same
Jesus which is taken up from you into heaven shall so
come in like manner as ye have seen Him go into
heaven" (Acts 1: 11). In bodily form, He has ascended;
in bodily form, He will come again. He has carried His
manhood up into heaven, and thrice He has appeared
to human eyes. Stephen, about to lay down his life as
the first martyr, "looked up steadfastly into heaven, and
saw . . . Jesus standing on the right hand of God" (Acts
7: 55). Saul of Tarsus, stricken to the ground in the
blaze of light, saw the Son of Man in all the splendour of
His divine glory (Acts 9: 5; 1 Cor. 15: 8). John the
Divine, in the Spirit on the Lord's Day, saw Him as
One Whose face was like the sun when it "shineth in his
strength" (Rev. 1: 16). And the proof that the Lord
Who will come is that "same Jesus" Who went into
heaven will lie in the scars of the Cross. The marks of
His Passion will never be effaced from His body, and
they are no doubt a source of wonder to the angels in
the presence of God. St. John beheld Him in the midst
of the throne as a Lamb that had been slain (Rev. 5: 6);
every eye shall see Him, and they also which pierced
Him when He comes again (Rev. 1: 7). Thus the reality
and the identity of His risen body are placed beyond

dispute and are full of comfort for all who lean upon His word: "For our conversation is in heaven, from whence also we look for the Saviour, the Lord Jesus Christ: Who shall change our vile body that it may be fashioned like unto His glorious body, according to the working whereby He is able even to subdue all things unto Himself" (Phil. 3: 20.21).

Chapter One

IT IS THE LORD

"After these things Jesus shewed Himself again to the disciples at the Sea of Tiberias; and on this wise shewed He Himself. There were together Simon Peter, and Thomas called Didymus, and Nathanael of Cana in Galilee, and the sons of Zebedee, and two other of His disciples. Simon Peter saith unto them, I go a fishing. They say unto him, We also go with thee. They went forth, and entered into a ship immediately; and that night, they caught nothing. But when the morning was now come, Jesus stood on the shore: but the disciples knew not that it was Jesus. Then Jesus saith unto them, Children, have ye any meat? They answered Him, No. And He said unto them, Cast the net on the right side of the ship, and ye shall find. They cast therefore, and now they were not able to draw it for the multitude of fishes. Therefore that disciple whom Jesus loved saith unto Peter, It is the Lord!"

JOHN 21 : 1.7.

St. John's plan had been to end his Gospel with the final words in chapter twenty; they had formed a noble climax in their statement about the Son of God and the gift of life through faith in His Name. Then he

took up his pen to add one more chapter as a kind of
postscript; no one can say how much later it was
written, but it is a delightful afterthought. The style
and the language make it clear that it was written by
the same hand, and the reason which led St. John to
add this new material to his record was the circulation
of a saying about himself (John 21 : 23). All the material
in this chapter is found in this Gospel alone, and it
transfers the scene and its events from Judaea to
Galilee. The words of the angel on the Resurrection
morning had sought to point the Twelve away from
Jerusalem: "Behold, He goeth before you into Galilee;
there shall ye see Him" (Matt. 28: 7). And this had
been confirmed by the words of the Lord Himself to
the women whom He met by the way: "Tell My
brethren that they go into Galilee, and there shall
they see Me" (Matt. 28: 10). Nothing would keep
them in Jerusalem but the solemnities of the Passover
Festival; this perhaps would account for the eight days
which were spent in the city after these words were
spoken. Then they made their way back to their home
in the north; there was a pause, and then we read:
AFTER THESE THINGS JESUS SHEWED HIMSELF AGAIN TO
THE DISCIPLES AT THE SEA OF TIBERIAS; AND ON THIS
WISE SHEWED HE HIMSELF. There were few notes of
time in the narrative of the forty days; the gaps between
the times when they saw Him were both wide and
empty. The phrase AFTER THESE THINGS is the usual
formula for the resumption of the narrative when
such a gap is found (cf. 3: 22; 5: 1; 6: 1; 7: 1). At
some time not clearly defined, perhaps within less than
two weeks of the Resurrection, the disciples were back

in Galilee, strengthened with the promise that there they would see Him.

The first emphasis in this narrative falls on those who were toiling on the sea: THERE WERE TOGETHER SIMON PETER, AND THOMAS CALLED DIDYMUS, AND NATHANAEL OF CANA IN GALILEE, AND THE SONS OF ZEBEDEE, AND TWO OTHER OF HIS DISCIPLES. Here were seven of the Twelve back in their old haunts, close to their old craft and calling, in Bethsaida of Galilee. Three were mentioned by name, and one new fact about Nathanael is brought to light; his home was in Cana, and this may throw further light on the Lord's visit to that village after He had first met Nathanael (cf. John 1:43.51; 2:1.11). Two were mentioned by their surname as "the sons of Zebedee", a less personal form of reference which was in keeping with St. John's reserve; the two brothers would have been named and placed next to Simon Peter had St. John not been the author. And there were two others who are not named but who are called "disciples". It has been thought that this means that they were not of the Twelve; but the use of the word "disciples" one verse before seems to refer to the Apostles. This must suggest that the word is now used again in the same sense, and it is not hard to surmise that they were none other than Andrew and Philip (cf. John 1:41; 1:43). Judas was now dead, and four were away, but no reason for their absence has been supplied. Perhaps they were not far away, for in that case there would have been no need to note that these disciples were now "together". Both the mention of the number of those who were present and the freedom from all anxious explanation about the absence of others fits in with the life-like reality of "this wonderful photograph by one who saw".[1] All was silent now on the mount and in the streets where He had taught, but they knew that He had risen; what would be more natural than that they should have come "together", perhaps in the home of Simon Peter?

We do not know how long they had to wait, but the suspense would make them long for some kind of activity: SIMON PETER SAITH UNTO THEM, I GO A FISHING. THEY SAY UNTO HIM, WE ALSO GO WITH THEE. THEY WENT FORTH AND ENTERED INTO A SHIP IMMEDIATELY; AND THAT NIGHT THEY CAUGHT NOTHING. Simon Peter was the leading spirit in this venture, true to his own instinct as a man of action. The brief exchange of plans and the immediate response is told with the effortless precision of one who had shared in it all. They did not know how or when He would come, and no plans had been formed for the future. The days were now passing by since they had last seen Him in Jerusalem and they only knew that they were to wait until He should appear. And out on the water, beneath the stars, plying their skill in their old trade, they could wait with quiet hope for His coming. The boat (τo $\pi\lambda o\tilde{\iota}o\nu$) and its tender ($\tau o$ $\pi\lambda o\iota\acute{a}\rho\iota o\nu$) were not far from Capernaum, and to think of them would bring no sense of discord. In that boat He had sailed; from its bow He had taught; in its stern He had slept.[2] Old memories would crowd their minds as they eased the boat out on to the deep. Here they had heard Him still the winds and calm the waves with words of power and had seen Him walking on the waters as if he were ashore. Most of them, if not all, had been born and bred by Galilee and were familiar with all its reefs and shoals; night was the most favourable time for fishing, and success was normal. But now, toil as they might, they took nothing; "that night", all their efforts were vain. The pronoun is emphatic (ἐν ἐκείνῃ τῇ νυκτί); it may imply that total failure was exceptional.[3] Their nets were let out and hauled in time and again; they were always empty.

It was just when disappointment was at its peak that the next step took place: BUT WHEN THE MORNING WAS NOW COME, JESUS STOOD ON THE SHORE: BUT THE DISCIPLES KNEW NOT THAT IT WAS JESUS. Westcott points out that the correct reading in the Revised Version affords a more vivid picture and is significant for our understanding of what followed: "When day was now breaking".[4] The pale light of dawn was spreading over the hills and their misty shadows were thrown across the lake. Jesus had come from some unknown quarter and was standing on the narrow strand of pebble and shell-strewn beach. We learn nothing as to where He had spent the night or the quarter from which He had now come, but we may glean from the evident solitude of the place that He now stood on the shore where the eastern hills rise towards Trachonitis.[5] There was enough light for the men in the boat to descry Him a hundred yards or so from the land, but His figure was too dim in that grey dawn for them to tell Who He was. They were so worn out with the toils of the night that morning found them wholly unexpectant. Busy perhaps with their last haul, listless with sheer fatigue, they "knew not that it was Jesus". But this is not a full explanation; this clause in the Greek text implies that their failure to know Him was both strange and surprising. It did not cross their minds that this solitary figure might be the Lord, for "their eyes were holden" (Luke 24: 16). They were preoccupied with toil, just as Mary and the Emmaus travellers had been preoccupied with grief; and they were no longer on the alert, or the first sight of that lonely Stranger on the shore would have made their hearts leap in recognition of Him.

The next emphasis in this narrative falls on Him Who was standing on the shore: THEN JESUS SAITH UNTO THEM, CHILDREN, HAVE YE ANY MEAT? THEY ANSWERED HIM, NO. The Lord at once took steps to forge contact with them by a question of the utmost simplicity. His voice would float across the calm waters, clear and articulate in the stillness of dawn, and His question was an easy way of putting Himself in touch with them as in the case of the disciples on the way to Emmaus (cf. Luke 24: 17). The word CHILDREN might indicate a difference in age or in social status rather than a closer tie of relationship; it would be used as we might use a word like LADS, and would convey the twin ideas of friendliness and interest. They looked tired and disappointed as they trailed the slack mesh behind the boat, and it was the kind of question that a friendly stranger might ask. Chrysostom understood the words as though He were asking if they had fish to sell;[6] but the Revised Version puts the question in its barest meaning: "Have ye aught to eat?" The word only suggests something to eat with bread, and this might well be fish (cf. John 6: 9). But the question was framed in a way which implied that they had met with no success: "So you have caught nothing?" And their reply at once came back over that calm stretch of water, the brief reply of tired boatmen. It was blunt; it was curt; it was just what weary men with empty nets would shout: No!

This was the great moment when He chose to make the truth known by words of self-revelation: AND HE SAID UNTO THEM, CAST THE NET ON THE RIGHT SIDE OF THE SHIP, AND YE SHALL FIND. THEY CAST THEREFORE, AND NOW THEY WERE NOT ABLE TO DRAW IT FOR THE MULTITUDE OF FISHES. There may have come to them a vague recollection that this had all happened in their experience before, but this command was as precise as the command on that earlier occasion had been broad and sweeping (cf. Luke 5: 4); and the definite character of the command helps to explain the absence of protest and the alacrity with which they now obeyed. The tired boatmen at once prepared to act as He enjoined almost as though His words had cast a spell over their minds; but the spell of omnipotence that was on them would move along natural avenues of motive and action. There was partly the non-resistance of fatigue; there was partly the faint hope of success. They may have thought that He could see a shoal of fish in the shallows to the right which they could not see from the water's level.[7] It is common enough for one boat to make a haul while others only a few yards away may take nothing at all; one may strike the shoal which others have missed. Such would be their feelings as they tried one last throw and let down their net on the right side of the ship. The result was immediate; it was heavy with fish. It is true that it was not so heavy that the net broke (John 21: 11;

cf. Luke 5: 6); yet they could not pull it into the ship. This is a small sign that shows how tired their hands must have been; all they could do in the end was to bring the boat to shore, dragging the net behind.[8]

This was enough to stir St. John's quick mind with swift insight as to the truth: THEREFORE THAT DISCIPLE WHOM JESUS LOVED SAITH UNTO PETER, IT IS THE LORD." Just as it was in the act of breaking bread that the two disciples had known Him in Emmaus, so now it was in this miraculous draught of fish that St. John knew that it was the Lord. This clear perceptive faculty helps to explain why he was the "disciple whom Jesus loved"; there was a bond of intuitive understanding at the heart of that unique friendship. Thus St. John saw nothing that he could not have seen before; he saw nothing which the others could not see just as well. But he read the meaning which lay within that sign; he knew that it spoke of Jesus. It was not as though his eyes were clearer than the eyes of others; it was simply that his love was far more vivid. That sign awoke his love with this conscious insight, and he knew that it was the Lord. He who had been first to grasp the significance of the empty tomb was first to know that solitary Stranger, and he turned to Simon Peter with the whispered words of recognition: IT IS THE LORD. He had become conscious of His identity in a flash of perfect insight, and he knew at once who it was; and he referred to Him, not as Jesus, but as THE LORD. It was Thomas who had taught them the use of that title for the One Who had burst the bands of death (John 20: 28).[9] St. John's use of the same title in this instinctive utterance shows how quickly it became "the habitual designation" of the Risen Saviour.[10]

The whole narrative resembles in character and circumstance a much earlier episode; there had been a miraculous draught of fish in the same Sea of Tiberias at the beginning of His ministry. That had been an event which was symbolical of their call to the new life of discipleship: "And when they had brought their ships to land, they forsook all and followed Him" (Luke 5: 11). And there was an inherent element of parable and prophecy in this Resurrection Sign as well as miracle and history; it sums up the way in which the Risen Lord still directs the work of His servants. He stands on the shore of Eternity while we still toil on the restless waters of Time, and His presence sheds a deep sense of peace across the seas of life like a moonbeam that shines upon the waves. He may allow us to toil in vain while we toil only in our own strength, but we should be alert to see His face and hear His voice in the midst of all our effort. To take Him at His word and to let down our net in the simplicity of faith is the one way in which to know the grand surprise of true success. Nothing else will teach His servants so gladly to exclaim: IT IS THE LORD.

Chapter Two

A FIRE OF COALS

"Now when Simon Peter heard that it was the Lord, he girt his fisher's coat unto him, (for he was naked,) and did cast himself into the sea. And the other disciples came in a little ship; (for they were not far from land, but as it were two hundred cubits,) dragging the net with fishes. As soon as they were come to land, they saw a fire of coals there, and fish laid thereon, and bread. Jesus saith unto them, Bring of the fish which ye have now caught. Simon Peter went up, and drew the net to land full of great fishes, an hundred and fifty and three: and for all there were so many, yet was not the net broken. Jesus saith unto them, Come and dine. And none of the disciples durst ask Him, Who are Thou? knowing that it was the Lord. Jesus then cometh, and taketh bread, and giveth them, and fish likewise. This is now the third time that Jesus shewed Himself to His disciples, after that He was risen from the dead."   JOHN 21: 7.14.

The first recorded utterance of St. John was at the outset of his discipleship: "Rabbi, where dwellest Thou?" (John 1: 38). His third and last saying in this Gospel was his whispered intimation: "It is the Lord" (John 21: 7). And the contrast between the word "Rabbi" when his discipleship began and the designa-

tion "the Lord" as a result of the Resurrection sums
up the whole dénouément of the Gospel. It is true to
all that we know of St. John to find him in the act of
sharing his great discovery; he could not keep it to
himself, but had to share it with Simon Peter. But
while vision might be enough for him, action was
imperative for Peter, and the narrative concentrates
on his movements: NOW WHEN SIMON PETER HEARD
THAT IT WAS THE LORD, HE GIRT HIS FISHER'S COAT
UNTO HIM, (FOR HE WAS NAKED,) AND DID CAST HIMSELF
INTO THE SEA. Two sides of his delightful character at
once came out in the scene thus described: he could
not sit idle in the ship when the Lord was on the shore;
yet he could not appear in His presence while in a near
naked state of undress. The word NAKED may be taken
as a relative description: he was less than half-clad,
wearing next to nothing, "stripped of all but his light
under-garment."[1] Therefore he caught up the outer
cloak which was worn on cold nights and in storms,
wrapped it round his body, and cast himself into the
sea; and then, half-swimming, half-wading, caring not
how, he strove to reach the Lord. To gird on such a
coat is the reverse of what we would expect in the case
of a man who was about to throw himself into the sea,
and no one but an eye-witness would ever have con-
ceived such an idea.[2] But the circumstances would
explain his action, and it was so like him. It was the
same instinctive reverence as when he had cried out
that he was too sinful to stand in His presence (Luke
5: 8); it was the same impulsive devotion as when he
had left the boat to meet Him walking on the water
(Matt. 14: 28).

Peter forgot fish and net and boat and friends in haste to be at His side: AND THE OTHER DISCIPLES CAME IN A LITTLE SHIP; (FOR THEY WERE NOT FAR FROM LAND, BUT AS IT WERE TWO HUNDRED CUBITS,) DRAGGING THE NET WITH FISHES. He left John and the five others to drop anchor, board the dinghy, and haul the net to shore. And yet we do not know that he was much before them in reaching the sand where the Lord stood; they were no great distance away, and it would not take long to beach the boat. "The ship" (το πλοῖν) and "the little ship" (το πλοιάριον) point to two distinct vessels; the same words were employed to make the same distinction when the disciples had put to sea after He fed the five thousand (John 6: 22). They must have made the main vessel fast by anchor, transferred to the small craft, secured the net behind, and then towed it, teeming with fish, to land. They jumped ashore but did not haul it in, for they were now on the tip-toe of a new-found wonder. Men who had been engaged all night in a common pursuit, alternating between hope and disappointment, toiling on hour by hour, and tired out by morning, were now alive with joy. They did not speak; the only word spoken had been St. John's word to Simon Peter: they were content to act in a silent concert of awe at the presence of the Risen Master.

All seven disciples were soon side by side on the shore, and their eyes were full of wonder: AS SOON THEN AS THEY WERE COME TO LAND, THEY SAW A FIRE OF COALS THERE, AND FISH LAID THEREON, AND BREAD. How did Simon Peter greet the Lord when he came ashore? Did the others speak to Him when they stood in His presence? We do not know; the words which may have been voiced are not told in this record. St. John proceeds at once to turn our thoughts to a new sight that met their eyes on the edge of the sea. There on the cold pebbles they saw a fire of coals and the food for a meal. There was "a fish"; there was "a loaf"; and that charcoal fire had been laid for the necessary preparation.[3] This was for the disciples like the prophet's experience in the wilderness: when he awoke beneath the tree where he had slept, he found "a cake baken on the coals and a cruse of water at his head" (1 Kings 19: 6). The whole scene was in the very spirit in which He had once fed the five thousand with five loaves and a few small fish. It was just what seven men, tired out with fruitless toil, wet through with hauling nets, hungry with the keen morning air, would stand most in need of. Nor was that all. There was mystery as well as miracle in that fire: from whence had it come? There was tenderness as well as providence in that meal: of Whom did it speak?

But though the fire was laid and the meal was ready, He would have them add to its fare: JESUS SAITH UNTO THEM, BRING OF THE FISH WHICH YE HAVE NOW CAUGHT. Plummer points out that there is an artless simplicity in the ensuing narrative which has its own value: this verse and the next four verses are all without any connecting particles (cf. John 20: 13.19).[4] Details are few and the tone is brief and reserved, but this is in keeping with a calm and accurate narrative. There is no wild statement of the fantastic; it is as far as can be from invention; and the very imperfections of the disciples are of value as the water-mark of a truthful account.

The style is so direct that it creates its own atmosphere of awed excitement. The Lord had yet more to impart before they were to break their fast. His words were quiet and few as He told them to bring of the fish which had just been caught. Such a command might seem a mere trifle on the part of One Who had now destroyed the power of death, but it was the mark of Him "Who in His mortal life had ever shewn Himself mindful of the needs of mortal men."[5] He was independent of them; He had procured that fire of coals, that fish and bread, without their aid. Yet He valued what they could bring; He would have them to be partners with Him. Just as the haul of fish had been secured partly through His guidance and partly through their own efforts, so this morning meal was furnished partly by Him and partly by themselves.[6]

Peter took charge once more, perhaps as the master of the ship, but also as one who was always first in action: SIMON PETER WENT UP AND DREW THE NET TO LAND FULL OF GREAT FISHES, AN HUNDRED AND FIFTY AND THREE: AND FOR ALL THERE WERE SO MANY, YET WAS NOT THE NET BROKEN. Peter got up and went aboard the ship to which the net was still fastened and which was now in shallow water. It was he who landed the net with its large haul, and the fish were laid out on the beach and counted as in the days of old. No doubt six pairs of hands beside his own would help to lay them out, and we can sense the thrill of their early calling as the catch was numbered. It was no mean haul by any standard and we can almost hear the fisherman's voice as he stood counting each fish in turn. There was nothing mystical in the figure that was given as the total: "an hundred and fifty and three"; it was stated with a simple precision because it was so clearly remembered. This was like the explicit reference to six water pots at Cana (John 2: 6) or to five loaves and two small fish and twelve baskets at the feeding of five thousand (John 6: 9.13). It was not just a round number; there was finality in both count and record. And the size of that haul with a single cast of the net led the writer to add one more vividly remembered detail; for in contrast with the earlier occasion and in spite of that great struggling mass of large fish, the net was not so much as torn.

Peter's task would soon be complete, and the Lord's voice was heard once more in the crisp air of that early morning: JESUS SAID UNTO THEM, COME AND DINE, AND NONE OF THE DISCIPLES DURST ASK HIM, WHO ART THOU? KNOWING THAT IT WAS THE LORD. When He had first appeared to them, it was behind closed doors; and to prove His reality to them, He had taken "a piece of . . . fish . . . and did eat before them" (Luke 24: 42.43). Now He stood on the shore, and there was no need to prove His reality again; but to remove all sense of strain from those whose hearts were full of awe, He now called them to come and eat. Perhaps the call to COME means that they were standing at a little distance, holding back with mingled awe and wonder. The word to DINE spoke of breakfast, a meal which was sometimes refused by men who were anxious to reach farm or market (Matt. 22: 4.5). But this invitation meant that He would approach the fire from the land-side as they from the lake-side; He would act as the host and they would be his guests. It would seem that they had fallen under the hush of a profound silence, and it was the silence of an unspoken reverence. No one dared to ask Who it was that called them to break their fast, because such asking would imply a doubt where no doubt could exist; it would have been irreverent to question or inquire when the truth was beyond all doubt. There had been no special declaration that it was He Himself (cf. Luke 24: 39), but they could not escape from the absolute certainty that this was the Risen Saviour. The long suspense was now over and the time of waiting was at an end; they were in His presence, and nothing else mattered. They could not know how He had come, but they knew that it was Jesus.

They were content to greet Him in silent wonder and to come in humble obedience: JESUS THEN COMETH, AND TAKETH BREAD, AND GIVETH THEM, AND FISH LIKEWISE. The sun came up over the hills and turned the grey waters to gold as He now came forward.[7] He would relieve the sense of awe in their minds as He took bread and fish and gave each his share; and the definite articles in the Greek text ("the bread . . . the fish") point back to the food which He had prepared before they had landed (cf. John 21: 9).[8] Was there only one loaf and one fish by that fire of coals, enough food for one man? Did it increase as He broke it in His hands and gave it to them? Nothing is said of the fish which they had been told to bring, neither are we told if the Lord Himself partook of that fish and that bread. It is enough to know that the Lord would preside at that frugal repast as He had done in the house at Emmaus. He was in the midst of seven plain men who stood on the pebbles by the lake-side after their night of toil, the One Who had risen after the power of an endless life in the midst of those who were mortal. Perhaps their sense of awe would be greater than on previous occasions, and no wonder; for each successive appearance would tell them that He was nearer to His glory.

St. John concludes this part of his account with a simple comment: THIS IS NOW THE THIRD TIME THAT JESUS SHEWED HIMSELF TO HIS DISCIPLES AFTER THAT HE WAS RISEN FROM THE DEAD. These words have no valid meaning unless they are taken in the context of the entire Johannine narrative; then they may be compared with the considered reference to the "beginning of miracles" in Cana of Galilee and "the second miracle that Jesus did when He was come out of Judaea into Galilee" (John 2: 11; 4: 54). St. John's statement must mean either that this was now the third day on which He appeared or that it was the third group to whom He appeared; and the latter alternative is the more probable. St. John himself had described His first appearance; it had been to Mary Magdalene: but the wording of this text makes it clear that we are to distinguish between His appearance to single persons and His appearance to the disciples as a body. St. John had told of His appearance to the disciples on two earlier occasions, and this was now THE THIRD TIME that He showed Himself to them. There were only two other group appearances of which we know, one on the hills of Galilee, one on the mount of Olivet, and they were both as yet in the future. And this third time that He appeared to the disciples was to have its special value

in their memories. It was this scene rather than that in
the upper room at Jerusalem or in the house at Emmaus
which lay behind Peter's vivid recollection as to how
they "did eat and drink with Him after He rose from
the dead" (Acts 10: 41). It is perhaps like a picture of
the heavenly festival which is to come. He will hale us
ashore when the morning of the day that knows no
end dawns at last, and we will leave the night and the
deep to stand in the full sunlight of His presence. And
there we shall hunger no more, neither thirst any more:
for the Divine Shepherd on the hills of glory will feed
us and will lead us beside living waters in that country
of our desire (Rev. 7: 16.17).

Chapter Three

LOVEST THOU ME?

"So when they had dined, Jesus saith to Simon
Peter, Simon, son of Jonas, lovest thou Me more
than these? He saith unto Him, Yea, Lord; Thou
knowest that I love Thee. He saith unto him, Feed
My lambs. He saith to him again the second time,
Simon, son of Jonas, lovest thou Me? He saith unto
Him, Yea, Lord, Thou knowest that I love Thee.
He saith unto him, Feed my sheep."

JOHN 21: 15.16.

There was silence in the hearts of those who stood
round that fire of coals when the frugal meal was over.
He that "turneth the shadow of death into the morning"
(Amos 5: 8) was the only One Who could break that
silence, and they waited with tense but quiet expectation. At last they heard Him speak, and it was as "the
Lord"; but while He spoke in the hearing of all, His
words were addressed to one in particular: SO WHEN
THEY HAD DINED, JESUS SAITH TO SIMON PETER. Peter was
thus singled out as if he were quite alone for a searching
exchange of questions and answers. Peter had been
active enough since the Lord had appeared on the shore
that morning: he had plunged into the water to swim
or wade to the lake-side; he had climbed back into the
beached tender to haul in the net and to count the fish.
But the Lord knew that such surface activity hid the

deep wound which had been left by that night of tears
and terror when he had turned his back with oath and
curse. The Lord had made Himself known to Peter in
a private capacity during the day on which He was
raised from the dead (Luke 24: 34); that special appearance was never forgotten, but no details have been
preserved (1 Cor. 15: 5). Peter had also been present
in the upper room in Jerusalem on both evenings, one
week apart, when the Lord had revealed Himself to
the disciples as a company, and had heard His greeting
of peace and His commission for their ministry. But his
lacerated conscience stood in need of something more
than private reconciliation or a general commission,
and the reassurance of a personal interview was to find
its sequel in an act of public reinstatement. The Lord
now dealt with him in the presence of six fellow disciples
and with the healing thrust of a searching tenderness.
It was a scene that would remind him of his fall and
his weakness in a way which would teach him to watch
and withstand.

The Lord began with a form of address which would
recall His first words at their first meeting more than
three years before: SIMON, SON OF JONAS, LOVEST THOU
ME MORE THAN THESE? It was the Lord Who had conferred on him the new name of Peter, yet He never
addressed him by that name except in one remarkable
instance (Luke 22: 34). St. John always gave him both
names, Simon Peter, except only when the surname
was first about to be conferred (John 1: 41). But here
the name Simon was amplified by reference to his father,
and this was by design. It would direct Peter's mind

back to that initial interview when the Lord had told
him: "Thou art Simon the son of Jona: thou shalt be
called Cephas" (John 1: 42). He was not yet that man
of rock, though his heart was that of a child; this was
neither Cephas nor Peter, but only Simon, son of Jonas,
as long ago. And the question was as elemental as the
appellation had been, although the phrase, MORE THAN
THESE, is ambiguous. It could refer to the boats and the
nets from which the Lord had first called him and in
the midst of which He had found him that day; it could
refer to the friends and brethren who were with him
and who had meant so much to him. And the tenor of
the question in each case would have been: Do you
love Me more than you love all these? But there can
be little doubt that the real intent was to probe his
heart in another direction: Do you love Me more than
these thy brethren love Me? Such words would stab
him to the quick. His old weakness had been to boast
of a superior love and devotion: though all should take
offence, he had declared, yet he would not (Matt.
26: 33; cf. John 13: 37). Never would he fail as others
might fail! Did he not love better than they? He had
been full of such hollow comparisons; they were always
in favour of himself. But he had failed when the crisis
had come, and his failure was now exposed by this
firm and searching question: Simon, son of Jonas, is
your love for Me purer, stronger, higher than theirs?[1]
Peter would not now dare to boast that he excelled
others in love; he would not now speak of others at all.
HE SAITH UNTO HIM, YEA, LORD; THOU KNOWEST THAT I
LOVE THEE. Peter's reply was a simple affirmative, but
stern experience had taught him to distrust his own

judgement.[2] The Lord knew what was in his heart, and he appealed to that direct insight. But there is a subtle contrast in the Greek text between the verbs "to love" which in English are both rendered by the same word, and the delicate shade of difference which this contrast involves throws its own light on the play of thought and feeling in this luminous dialogue. The Lord chose a word[3] which implies the idea of respect, and so conveys the thought of choice: "LOVEST thou Me?" Such a love is born of understanding; it is love in its most lofty form of pure and reverent devotion. Did he cherish a love like this, a love that sprang from clear moral insight? But he would not make such a claim and the word which he chose[4] was in emphatic avoidance of the Lord's word: "Thou knowest that I LOVE Thee." This was a less exalted devotion than that to which the Lord's word had pointed, for that was still beyond his heart; it spoke of an honest, humble, personal affection, something of which he could feel sure. It is only when the two words occur side by side as in this passage that these shades of meaning stand out clearly. Peter could not rise to the height of a love so rich and serene as the Lord's word implied; he felt poor and incapable. So he replied with that other word, full of warm human feeling: "I love Thee with such love as this poor heart can feel;"[5] I love Thee as a man may love his friend.

The strong emotional currents released by question and answer were all at last compelled to flow in a single channel: HE SAITH UNTO HIM, FEED MY LAMBS. The Lord did not say in reply what might have been hoped for: "Yea, I know that thou dost love Me."[6] His words were in fact as gentle as words could be, but there was a significant development. They would restore poise and purpose to a troubled spirit. Their aim in this respect may be compared with that of the command which was laid on Mary outside the tomb (John 20: 17). Peter had not ventured on any rash promise for the future; it was as though he could only trust himself to speak of the present. But the Risen Saviour brought the future into sight at once with this charge to feed the lambs of that flock which He had purchased with His own blood (Acts 20: 28). He who was first called to be a fisher of men was now called to be a shepherd of souls; he recovered the commission which he had lost when he denied the Lord. The old calling had been to do the work of an evangelist; this new concern was for the work of a pastor. The whole phrase, FEED MY LAMBS, speaks of tender concern for "the very weak and the very young", for all who are "lamb-like" in the flock of that great Shepherd.[7] It points to the humblest aspect of a shepherd's duty: to feed them, give them food, and lead them among green pastures and beside still waters. Such a shepherd, Peter was to become.

Perhaps a short pause would follow that first exchange between the Lord and His servant; it was the Lord Who then broke the silence: HE SAITH TO HIM AGAIN THE SECOND TIME, SIMON, SON OF JONAS, LOVEST THOU ME? He asked the same question in the same words except that the final phrase, "more than these", was dropped. Peter had thus gained a little; there was no thought now of comparison with his brethren. But the fundamental question was still the same, and its thrust was still more direct in the absence of comparison with others. He refrained from comment on the word which Peter had used, but there was a distinctive emphasis in the original word which He now retained. Do you only feel for Me what any man may feel for his friend? Or have you made your choice and fixed your heart above all else on Me? This quiet penetrating question insists on the primary importance of love. It was Simon Peter who had confessed his faith in a historic utterance (Matt. 16: 16); but the Lord did not ask him now: Dost thou believe? It was Simon Peter who had pledged his obedience in a vehement assertion (Luke 22: 33); but the Lord did not ask him now: Wilt thou obey? Faith and obedience were both absorbed in love, and the only thing that mattered was that Peter who had denied Him should learn to confess his love. He asked because He cared, and the fact that He cared gave His words a richer meaning: "Simon, son of Jonas, thou art the man I love; lovest thou Me?"

Peter's reply was in the same words as before; he did love Him, but he could not match the word which the Lord had used: HE SAITH UNTO HIM, YEA, LORD, THOU KNOWEST THAT I LOVE THEE. Peter, rugged, manly, headstrong, could not escape from that searching question in the morning sunlight. He could not close his heart to that persistent emphasis on a love that transcends all man's earthly passions. There was indeed nothing incongruous in such a claim from such a source; it was one of the more profound indications of His oneness with the Father. Did his love draw its strength from the choice of a soul that was fired with the love of God? Humility made him shrink from a test that was still too high and lofty. His love was the warm and kindly feeling of a heart that feels for a friend, and it was a guileless instinct that led him to use the right word for a chastened spirit. In long after years, he could speak without reserve of this same Lord as the One "Whom having not seen, ye love" (1 Peter 1 : 8).[8] But here, by the lake and the fire, he would claim no more than a love of which he could be sure: a love with less of choice or insight than that for which the Lord had asked; a love with more of warmth and feeling in a spirit that was true to himself.

There was development in thought and a change in the text of the words in reply: HE SAITH UNTO HIM, FEED (TEND, R.V.) MY SHEEP. The lambs were to be fed; the sheep would need even more care. They had to be tended by the shepherd, guided by day, folded by night, and watched over in all weather and all circumstances. It is unwise to mark off the lambs from the sheep with an over-rigid line of demarcation; both lambs and sheep belong to the one flock, and they describe what the divine Shepherd of souls sees in us all. There are the lambs, helpless and immature; there are the sheep, foolish and credulous: but He knows them all, and they hear His voice. And the Lord had work for Peter to do; he was to tend these sheep. That would require all the self-denial, patience and tenderness that true love could command. It is interesting to think how John Bunyan placed four Shepherds on the Delectable Mountains and named them with homely significance; they refreshed the pilgrims and sent them on their way with fresh joy in their hearts and a far-off vision before their eyes. And now Simon Peter

D

was to prove what manner of love was in his heart by the way in which he would tend the sheep. It was as though the Lord had said: Thou canst not now welcome Me in thy home, lend Me thy boat, or guard Me with thy sword; but by thy love for Me, feed My lambs, tend My sheep, care for that flock for which I gave My life and died.

There stood the Lord face to face with Peter by the lake-side, near the fish and the fire, in the clean light of a new day; and that question had been twice asked and twice answered in the hearing of six others. The night on the lake was over; its lassitude and excitement had passed. The Lord's words were few but searching, spoken with quiet voice and divine authority; Peter's stirring spirit was now subdued, and his feelings restrained. It was perhaps the most moving moment in his life of crowded activity. The sun that shone on his face was not half so real as the fire that burned in his heart. He would never forget those words: LOVEST THOU ME? It is true that there are many ways in which love may be declared. It may be in silent worship, like that of the faithful women (Matt. 28: 9); it may be in ardent wonder, like that of the doubting Thomas (John 20: 28). Peter was by nature full of eager impulse and exuberant enthusiasm, but now he was subdued. He could only speak with chastened sincerity: THOU KNOWEST THAT I LOVE THEE. And those sober words meant far more than his boastful sayings of old. They touch reality; they bring out the true man; they do not hide his faults, but they make it clear that he loved Him.

Chapter Four

THOU KNOWEST ALL THINGS

"He saith unto him the third time, Simon, son of
Jonas, lovest thou Me? Peter was grieved because
He said unto him the third time, Lovest thou Me?
And he said unto Him, Lord, Thou knowest all
things; Thou knowest that I love Thee. Jesus saith
unto him, Feed My sheep."   JOHN 21:17.

The questions and answers in this momentous interview
in the early morning were not yet at an end. Three
times in all the Lord was to ask that question, and a
third time Peter had to reply. Not one word was said
with regard to things that were now in the past, but
that thrice asked question was an undoubted reference
to Peter's thrice repeated denial. St. John's Gospel
contains its own vivid account of that dark hour in the
hall of Caiaphas. "Verily, verily," Jesus had said, "the
cock shall not crow till thou hast denied Me thrice"
(John 13:38). And so it came to pass. Three times, to
the maiden at the door, to the servant by the fire, to
the kinsman of Malchus, with oath, with curse, with
vehement blasphemy and resolute denial, he had sworn
to a lie: "I know not what thou sayest; I do not know
the man" (Matt. 26:70, 72, 74). But the heart of
Jesus was as full of love as ever, and as the cock began

to crow, He had turned and looked on Peter (Luke
22: 61). It was a look that broke his heart; he had
gone out into the night and wept. He would never
forget that long night of awful darkness and those tears
of blinding sorrow. But that failure in the hall of
Caiaphas was now redeemed by the sea of Galilee,
and the words which had scarred his soul were now
submerged in words of love.

The Lord well knew what grave trouble of mind had
held him in torment since that dark night before the
Cross. Therefore after a pause He spoke again: HE
SAITH UNTO HIM THE THIRD TIME, SIMON, SON OF JONAS,
LOVEST THOU ME? It was true that the Lord had seen
Peter alone towards evening on the day on which He
rose from the grave (Luke 24: 34). Their conversation
is unrecorded; it was private because it was sacred.
The Lord must have restored His now deeply penitent
disciple to forgiveness and fellowship, or it would be
impossible to explain the silence of the Gospels on
this question. But confession and forgiveness which
took place in private would not protect Peter from all
uneasy misgivings in the presence of his brethren
because his failure had taken place in public. There
had been a hint of uneasiness in the impulsive violence
with which he had jumped out of the ship and begun
to wade ashore. It was conduct in which a trace of
self-display and a longing for some open recognition
were the hidden, perhaps only half-understood, motives.
Self-assertive impulse and an unspeakable sadness may
at times and in some natures lie close to each other,
and there was room for both in the complexities of this

man's heart. Peter was never more sober-minded than in that calm morning sunlight beside the sea, and this continued dialogue in the presence of six others was meant to meet his most urgent need through reinstatement in his apostolic calling.

Thus for the third time the Lord asked him that searching question in words which could not lose their grave appeal: SIMON, SON OF JONAS, LOVEST THOU ME? He would not drag up that sin for mention by name in the hearing of his brethren, but the significance of the thrice asked question would be clear to them all. He was content to ask for a positive confession of love, leaving it to conscience to make reply. But there was a change in the form of His question; He dropped His own word, twice used,[1] in favour of the word which Peter had used.[2] He had given up the thought of comparison with his brethren after the first time of asking, and now He went even further; He gave up the lofty ideal of love which His own word required and came right down to the level which Peter had chosen. It meant that He was now willing to take Peter at his own self-valuation, and to meet him on his own ground, and to test the reality of the love which he did profess. We may expand the text to bring out in full each shade of meaning.[3] "I note the word which you prefer," this would imply; "I understand your choice. And now I am content to take your word and re-phrase My question. I do not ask now if you love Me with the pure exalted devotion of a saint for his God; I ask only whether you love Me with the true personal affection of a man for his friend. LOVEST THOU ME?"

But this question in its new form touched his wound on the raw: PETER WAS GRIEVED BECAUSE HE SAID UNTO HIM THE THIRD TIME, LOVEST THOU ME?" It would be a humbling experience for this head-strong, impulsive disciple to find himself questioned like this in the hearing of his six friends, but his reply to the first two questions had been grave and modest in tone, without sign of undue distress or of harassed feeling. But he was grieved, and could not hide his grief, when the question was asked again; it broke through the strength of his own inner reserve and brought to the surface all the hidden sorrow of his own heart. He may have grieved partly because he was asked the same thing for THE THIRD TIME; the three times of asking could not fail to remind him of the three separate acts of denial. But it was not only the fact that the question was put to him again; it was as well the fact that THE THIRD TIME the word which had been used before was changed.[4] He grieved because the choice of his own word for that question in this third and final challenge seemed to imply some doubt whether he could even rightly claim that humble form of love which he had affirmed. He knew only too well that his record in the past might give cause for doubt: who could be sure of his earnest declaration of love, even though it were made without boastful comparison with others and without reckless promise for the future.[5] The probe had done its work; he was now both GRIEVED and truly ready to make his last reply.

Peter could not remain silent when that skilful, patient question searched all his heart. Therefore with

grief that lay too deep for tears he made reply: AND
HE SAID UNTO HIM, LORD, THOU KNOWEST ALL THINGS;
THOU KNOWEST THAT I LOVE THEE. This third question
and the reply put it beyond all doubt that the point
at issue turned on the use of the two words for love.
It owes its force to the contrast between the two ideas
of love conveyed in the two words which had been
used: the one spoke of the calm pure choice of an
informed mind, while the other spoke of the strong
warm love of a feeling heart. Bishop Moule asks
whether this clear verbal contrast may be taken as an
incidental proof that the Lord sometimes conversed
with the Twelve in the Greek lingua franca of the
Roman Empire rather than the Aramaic vernacular
of Galilee and Judaea. He points to the fact that
Aramaic has no parallel distinction of verbs, and he
concludes that the language of this conversation must
have been Greek.[6] Peter therefore framed his reply in
words which would engage the point which had been
raised, and his answer had the ring of artless, spontaneous simplicity.

It was utterly convincing: LORD, THOU KNOWEST
ALL THINGS; THOU KNOWEST THAT I LOVE THEE. He
had always been quick to speak, and some of the finest
sayings in the Gospel records were his. It was Peter
who in response to a wistful question at Capernaum
had said: "Lord, to whom shall we go? Thou hast the
words of eternal life" (John 6: 68). It was Peter who
in response to a searching question at Caesarea Philippi
had said: "Thou art the Christ, the Son of the living
God" (Matt. 16: 16). But this reply excels them all
in the transparent character of its tender humility and

its utter sincerity. Peter dropped the exclamation, "yea, Lord", with which he had begun before, and threw himself still more decisively on the Master's knowledge of his own heart as well as of "all things". He used two words which in English are both rendered by the same word: "Thou KNOWEST (οἶδας) all things; Thou KNOWEST (γινώσκεις) that I love Thee." There had been a similar transition from the first word to the second in more than one context in this Gospel (cf. John 7: 27; 13: 7; and in reverse, 8: 55; 14: 7). The first, THOU KNOWEST, was an appeal to divine intuition, while the second, THOU SEEST, was an appeal to personal discernment. Peter appealed from His universal knowledge which would include "all things" to His special insight in his own case: Thou Who knowest all things canst see at this very moment that I love Thee. And if his word for love was more lowly than the word which the Lord had used at first, it was only so by comparison and in itself still affirmed a love that was deep and warm and full of tender human feeling.

Then for the third time the Lord laid on him the charge: HE SAITH UNTO HIM, FEED MY SHEEP. Lambs which can not travel in their own strength scarcely stand in need of guidance; their great need is for food. The sheep need both, and the shepherd has to feed as well as tend the flock. The Lord remained the chief Shepherd; they were "MY lambs"; "MY sheep". "I know MY sheep and am known of MINE" (John 10: 14). Peter's task would be that of an undershepherd in the care of that flock for which He had laid down His life. His thrice repeated confession of love had been followed by this now thrice repeated commission to serve, and he was to recall its terms in the charge which he in turn laid on the elders in his old age: "Feed the flock of God which is among you, taking the oversight thereof, not . . . as being lords over God's heritage, but being ensamples to the flock: and when the chief Shepherd shall appear, ye shall receive a crown of glory that fadeth not away" (1 Peter 5: 2.4). And it recalls with great power the glorious prophecy of the Messianic Servant: "He shall feed His flock like a shepherd: He shall gather the lambs with His arm, and carry them in His bosom, and shall gently lead those that are with young" (Isa. 40: 11).

It is remarkable that so little is found in the Scriptures about man's love for God. God's love for us shines in letters of gold: our love for God hardly finds a mention at all. And yet, love in return for love there must be if our hearts are true: "We love Him because He first loved us" (1 John 4: 19). But this moving confession of love by this chastened disciple is unique in Scripture: LORD, THOU KNOWEST ALL THINGS: THOU KNOWEST THAT I LOVE THEE. Canon Charles Smyth quotes a saying from a book called *Ara Coeli* to this effect: "Experience of God in this life means more than seeing a friend face to face, and less than seeing God face to face."[7] Then he adds his own true comment: "It is closer and more spiritual than the former, but more imperfect and fragmentary than the latter."[8] This may partly explain, though it can not excuse, our want of love and our coldness of heart. We need to be more like William Grimshaw who would often exclaim: "My God, my Jesus, I love Thee indeed; but how shall

I love Thee enough?"[9] If we can not speak like Simon Peter, we may nevertheless cry like Richard Baxter: "Though I can not say Thou knowest that I love Thee, yet can I say, Lord, Thou knowest that I WOULD love Thee."[10]

Chapter Five

WHEN THOU SHALT BE OLD

"Verily, verily, I say unto thee, When thou wast young, thou girdedst thyself, and walkedst whither thou wouldest: but when thou shalt be old, thou shall stretch forth thy hands, and another shall gird thee, and carry thee whither thou wouldest not. This spake He, signifying by what death he should glorify God. And when He had spoken this, He saith unto him, Follow Me."

JOHN 21: 18.19.

There was silence while the Lord stood on the pebbled shore in the midst of those disciples by the Sea of Galilee. Perhaps a light breeze would fan their cheeks as the sun began to climb above the hills. The small fishing vessel had been drawn up from the water, and the nets lay near-by, and the great haul of fish, and the embers of the fire, and the remnants of the meal. Simon Peter had been reinstated in the circle of His love and service with words which have never lost their memorable solemnity, and a pause of deliberate value may have followed the last exchange of question and answer, crowned by the charge to feed His sheep. Then the Lord spoke again, still with Peter alone in view, but still in the hearing of his fellows. The man who was to tend His flock would die for Him as well;

a good shepherd would lay down his life for the sheep.
Peter may not have been wholly aware of all that his
own words involved, but he had more than once
declared that he would face prison or death itself in
his Master's service. It was Peter who had asked Him
on the night when He was betrayed: "Lord, whither
goest Thou?" The Lord had told him in reply: "Whither
I go, thou canst not follow Me now; but thou shalt
follow Me afterwards". And Peter had answered:
"Lord, why can not I follow Thee now? I will lay
down my life for Thy sake" (John 13: 36.37). That
bold promise would be redeemed in full: the end result
of his discipleship would be nothing less than violent
martyrdom.

The Lord prefaced what He had to say with the old
familiar formula: VERILY, VERILY, I SAY UNTO THEE,
WHEN THOU WAST YOUNG, THOU GIRDEDST THYSELF
AND WALKEDST WHITHER THOU WOULDEST. The emphasis and gravity of the opening formula were in keeping
with the solemn sequence of thought. There was latent
drama in the tacit contrast between Peter's impetuous
manhood in full strength and vigour and the violent
death by which he would glorify God. His strong
impulsive qualities had been in the foreground of the
activities of that morning and were the key to his
virtues as well as his failings. A hint from John had
been enough to make him leave fish, nets and boat in
the attempt to wade through the waters and be the
first to reach the shore. A hint from the Lord had made
him spring up, drag the net from the sea, count the
haul one by one, and bring the fish that were needed.

He had been born and bred to the free and independent life of a boat master who sailed and fished at will, and he had just begun to taste its joys again. For him to think or to wish was to act, and his was zeal the Lord would not repress. Perhaps the Lord would look on him with eyes full of kindness, as a father who has passed through the world's darkest corners looks on a child's eager expectancy. And He would speak as one who had endured the Cross, seeking now to brace an impulsive disciple for the unknown sharpness of pain and death.

WHEN THOU WAST YOUNG, THOU GIRDEDST THYSELF AND WALKEDST WHITHER THOU WOULDEST: Plummer treats the first clause as though it read: "When thou wast younger than thou art now."[1] This would be a contrast between what he had been and what at that moment he was. Bishop Moule however treats the clause as proleptical; it looks back as it were to that moment from the time of his death. Peter was seen from the stand-point of the future and was described as he was that morning. The same usage is found in St. Paul's statement: "Then shall I know even as I am known" (1 Cor. 13: 12).[2] Peter and the others were much of an age with Himself; perhaps they were no more than thirty-five years old at most. Thus as Peter stood there, he was still a young man; strong, free, and in his prime. He could gird his own loins, as he had girt his cloak about him that very morning (John 21: 7). He could go whither he would, as when he had cast himself into the sea. He could choose his own path, and could follow it with manly vigour. But the freedom of youth would pass away, and the very form of those words would stress the fact that he would not always be as he was at that moment.

BUT WHEN THOU SHALT BE OLD, THOU SHALT STRETCH FORTH THY HANDS, AND ANOTHER SHALL GIRD THEE, AND CARRY THEE WHITHER THOU WOULDEST NOT: He would live to be old; but the contrast between youth and age was only incidental to the major contrast between the freedom he enjoyed as a young man and the restraint to which he was destined when he was old. A change would come when he could no longer do as he pleased but would have to submit to the will of others. He would stretch out his hands as one who was helpless and would appeal for help; stretch them out like a man who stands arraigned before the judge and can not stave off the judgement. Someone else would gird him, load him with chains, bind him as a felon condemned to die. Other hands would carry him to a goal which no man would choose for himself, would drive him out to the place of execution. It was not that he would refuse to die, but that human nature would shrink from such a death: the Lord Himself had not refused the cup, but had recoiled from all its dregs (Matt. 26: 39). It was right that Peter should choose the Lord and be willing to die rather than to deny His Name; but to choose death or pain for its own sake would have been an act of mental aberration.[3] Westcott points out that a violent death is always terrible because it is non-natural; and terrible in proportion to the element of that violence by which it is achieved.[4] Thus the contrast was as clear as words could portray: Peter as a young man had been so quick, strong and impetuous, full of nervous life and energetic action; but his old age would bring bonds and imprisonment and a violent martyrdom.

How would Simon Peter explain those words? St. John applied them to his death: THIS SPAKE HE, SIGNIFYING BY WHAT DEATH HE SHOULD GLORIFY GOD. This brief comment forms a parenthesis in the record of the conversation and is quite in the style of this Gospel (cf. John 2: 21; 7: 39; 12: 33; 18: 32). St. John had cast back in his mind to the point of time when the Lord had voiced that grave warning, and the verb was in the appropriate tense to describe something which was then still in the future.[5] The words had been enigmatic at the time when they were spoken, but their meaning had been made clear by the time when St. John wrote this account. He could explain their full significance as a result of the event: Simon Peter was dead; he had glorified God by suffering the death of a martyr at the cruel hands of men. The Lord had not declared by what manner of death he was to die, and it is a mistake to treat His words as though they were meant to foretell death by crucifixion. But there is no reason to doubt that he was in fact put to death on a cross just outside the great city of Rome. Tertullian was the first to affirm that for him the *via lucis* was the *via crucis*; Origen's tradition that at his own request he was crucified head downwards is less certain.

THIS SPAKE HE, SIGNIFYING BY WHAT DEATH HE SHOULD GLORIFY GOD: Peter may not have been able to grasp the full significance of that saying; it was enough that he should know in broad terms what it meant. Its full meaning would only be disclosed when

the events foretold took place, but he knew that it
spoke of long service and the crown of ultimate martyrdom. This was never far from his mind as the future
unrolled, and it sheds a warm ray of light on his state
of mind when under the threat of death at the hands of
Herod. He lay between the two soldiers, handcuffed
by each wrist to his guards, in full expectation that he
would be executed in the morning; but he slept like a
child (Acts 12: 6). The Lord's warning had not robbed
life of its value, but had strengthened faith in prospect
of the evil to come. This is made clear in his own words
to those who were also called to endure persecution.
"I think it meet as long as I am in this tabernacle,"
he wrote, "to stir you up by putting you in remem-
brance; knowing that shortly I must put off this my
tabernacle, even as our Lord Jesus Christ hath shewed
me" (2 Peter 1: 13.14). As long as he was free to
choose, he would tread the path of faith and obedience;
when he could no longer choose for himself, he would
accept what God had planned for him in love. This
was the sane outlook of one who would avoid a cruel
death while he could rightly do so, and yet of one
who knew that it would come at last. And this sober
realism would add authority to his martyr-witness
when the hour came.[6]

AND WHEN HE HAD SPOKEN THIS, HE SAITH UNTO
HIM, FOLLOW ME: St. John's parenthesis was at an end,
and the narrative of that interview was at once resumed.
It would seem that as soon as the Lord had voiced that
warning, He turned round and began to move away;
and as He went, He called Peter to leave his friends in
the group near the fire and to follow. It is not clear

why He did this; but the literal following would not
obscure the fact that this was the old call. That call
had been heard by Philip (John 1 : 43), by Peter and
Andrew (Matt. 4 : 19), and by Matthew (Matt. 9 : 9);
they had left all, their duties, their parents, their
occupations, to obey that call. There were others who
found that call hard to accept (Matt. 8 : 22; 19 : 21),
for it required them to follow mysterious paths which
led to disgrace and death (Matt. 10 : 38; 16 : 24). But
the old call would take on a new and larger meaning
as a result of His death and resurrection. It would
demand skill to perceive His ways and to discern His
will; then it would need courage to step out and follow
a path that might lead on to death.[7] This was just what
Peter had lacked during the days before the Lord's
death on the Cross: but it would now become the real
test of his love; he was called to follow, and that would
mean to lay down his life for Jesus' sake.

It is fitting at this point to recall the "*quo vadis*" legend
which St. Ambrose records. The facts are by no means
certain, but the story illustrates the truth with a
luminous pathos. Simon Peter had been condemned
in the city of Rome and was waiting to die; but friends
implored him to seize the chance for escape. That
would have been no crime: had not the Lord sent an
angel to save him from Herod? And he stole out
through the prison door to make once more for freedom
by the Via Appia. But as Peter, now an old man,
passed through the gate of the city in the grey light
of dawn, he met the Lord on His way in. "*Domine,
quo vadis?*" he cried; "Lord, whither goest Thou?"

E

And he then heard the Lord reply: "I go to be crucified in thy place." Peter was grieved at that saying; and he returned to his prison that by his death he might glorify God. Did he die on the site where the church of S. Pietro in Montorio now stands? Was he crucified head downwards as one who was scarcely worthy to die for Him? It may have been; but it does not matter.[8] It is enough to know that the God of all grace called him to stand in the glory of His presence after he had suffered a while (1 Pet. 5: 10).

Chapter Six

FOLLOW THOU ME

"Then Peter, turning about, seeth the disciple whom Jesus loved following; which also leaned on His breast at supper and said, Lord, which is he that betrayeth Thee? Peter seeing him saith to Jesus, Lord, and what shall this man do? Jesus saith unto him, If I will that he tarry till I come, what is that to thee? Follow thou Me. Then went this saying abroad among the brethren, that that disciple should not die: yet Jesus said not unto him, He shall not die; but, If I will that he tarry till I come, what is that to thee?"

JOHN 21:20.23.

The command to follow may have been meant, at least in part, as a figure of speech; but the tense of the verb and the context as a whole both show that there was movement as well. The Lord began to walk away from the circle of friends towards the line of hills or down the shore beside the sea. Peter then began to follow, thinking perhaps that there was more which still remained to be said in private. But John at once rose up and went after them while the others lingered near the fire. Was this a mark of John's intimacy with both Peter and his Master? Was the silence of the other five a sign of their own understanding and care in this deeply human situation? The whole narrative is drawn from the wells of personal memory and is full of life and movement. It affords a valuable insight into the life of these men and the mind of the Master. Each was called to follow: but the way was not the same and the ends were far apart. The character and destiny of God's servants are known to Him in such a way that they may look up with unfailing confidence like the Psalmist and say: "Thou shalt guide me with Thy counsel, and afterward receive me to glory" (Ps. 73 :24).

Peter had begun to follow the Lord but he was soon aware that they were not alone: THEN PETER, TURNING ABOUT, SEETH THE DISCIPLE WHOM JESUS LOVED FOLLOW-ING. He knew that he alone had been called to follow, but there were steps not far behind. Peter heard the footsteps, turned round, and was surprised to see John close at hand. John's name is not mentioned; he is simply described by an epithet as THE DISCIPLE WHOM JESUS LOVED. He is always anonymous in this Gospel, but reveals his identity in this phrase of grateful acknowledgement. It is found twice in the Passion narrative (John 13: 23; 19: 26) and twice in this chapter (21: 7,20), and it also occurs once in slightly altered language in a context in which Peter is joined with him (John 20: 2). The bond between Peter and John had been strengthened in a growing friendship since the Passion. They had lodged in the same house at Jerusalem (John 20: 10); they had run side by side to the tomb in Joseph's garden (John 20: 4); they had gone out to fish in the same boat on the waters of Galilee (John 21: 2). No one had been closer to the fallen Peter

in the darkness after his thrice repeated denial; no one
would have more right to be with him in the hour of
restoration. Since he was the favourite disciple of Jesus
Himself and the intimate companion of Peter as well,
what could be more true to human nature than that he
should also rise and follow?

WHICH ALSO LEANED ON HIS BREAST AT SUPPER AND
SAID, LORD, WHICH IS HE THAT BETRAYETH THEE? We
may wonder why this particular detail should be singled
out for mention. Perhaps it was partly because this was
the first occasion on which reference was made to "the
disciple whom Jesus loved" (John 13: 23). That would
have been explanation enough; but there seem to have
been other reasons as well. The emphasis is thrown on
what he did rather than on where he sat at table: he
was so close to the Lord that he could lean back and ask
in a whisper who the traitor could be. This had taken
place at the last supper after He had announced that a
traitor was then at the table. There was consternation
as each man searched his own heart and then asked
aloud: "Lord, is it I?" (Matt. 26: 22). Even Judas had
been shamed into asking: "Master, is it I?" And Jesus
had replied: "Thou has said" (Matt. 26: 25). But He
must have spoken in soft tones which only Judas could
hear, and this means that Judas must have reclined next
to Him on His left. No one else had heard this whispered
exchange and the suspense became unbearable. At last
Peter could stand it no longer and he made signs to
John who was on His right to ask who it was. And John
leant back and asked: "Lord, who is it?" (John 13: 25).
Perhaps no one except the Lord heard that question,
nor would any but John hear the reply. That scene is

now recalled because it had revealed the close understanding between Peter and John, and so explains why
John had now ventured to follow without a special
summons.

PETER SEEING HIM SAITH TO JESUS, LORD, AND WHAT
SHALL THIS MAN DO? It was so like Peter that his thoughts
should flash from his own future to that of John who
was now just behind; he may have found relief from
deep embarrassment in this attempt to turn further
conversation towards his friend. At all events, his quick,
impulsive reaction to John's presence was to ask the
question: LORD, AND WHAT SHALL THIS MAN DO? Westcott points out that the original text is singularly brief
and pregnant: "Lord, and this man, what?"[1] What
will happen to him? And what shall be his lot? Shall he
also grow old, and then stretch out his hands, and be
loaded with chains, and made to go where he fain
would not go?[2] He had started out in Peter's footsteps
as had Peter in the steps of Jesus: would he also follow
in the manner of his life and in the terror of his death
on a cross? This was much more than an idle, selfish,
curious inquiry; it sprang from an active, eager, natural
interest in the welfare of a devoted companion. The
fact that John was there at all raised a tacit question
as to what would become of him: did the future hold
the same end in store for both alike?

The Lord's reply was an emphatic assertion of His
own sovereign dignity and a definite correction of a too
familiar inquiry: JESUS SAITH UNTO HIM, IF I WILL THAT
HE TARRY TILL I COME, WHAT IS THAT TO THEE?
FOLLOW THOU ME. It is strange that Peter should need

reproof for an ill-timed remark just after his restoration
by the Sea of Galilee much as he had needed it after his
declaration of faith at Caesarea Philippi (Matt. 16: 23).
He craved to be conspicuous, but could not bear what
it entailed: it brought a false sense of self-importance,
and that always led to trouble.[3] This is at least partly
why the reply was so reserved: it was not for Peter to
know what God had in store for others. The IF veils the
divine purpose while the I WILL states the divine
authority: it was enough for him to know that the
divine will would rule John's future as it would rule his
own. The word TARRY is the correlative of the call to
FOLLOW and points to a patient continuance in life until
further light is revealed (cf. John 12: 35; Phil. 1: 25).[4]
The phrase TILL I COME should read WHILE I AM COMING,
and the leading idea is that of an interval of waiting
rather than an end to be reached.[5] But the ultimate
emphasis falls on the three pronouns, HIM, THOU, and
ME. Peter's concern for John's future was in effect beside
the point; his own welfare would be better served by
personal following: "What I will for him is of no concern to thee: and as for thee, follow Me; that is all."

THEN WENT THIS SAYING ABROAD AMONG THE BRETHREN
THAT THAT DISCIPLE SHOULD NOT DIE: The Lord's reply
soon became a familiar tradition among those who were
known as THE BRETHREN. The way had been prepared
for the use of this name by the Lord's words to the
Twelve (Matt. 23: 8), to Simon Peter (Luke 22: 32),
and to Mary in the garden (John 20: 17), and it was to
become common in The Acts as a name for the believing
community (Acts 9: 30; 11: 1,29; 15: 1,3,22, etc.). But
this is the only place where it is employed in a formal

manner in the Gospels, and it reflects a new sense of fellowship among the disciples after the Resurrection.[6] The Lord's saying was to mould the ideas of that generation on the subject of John's future with a misleading sense of mystery. It was construed as though the phrase TILL I COME was meant to mark His Second Coming and the Age of Immortality rather than the time of waiting before that great Advent. Thus they argued that John was not to die; he would remain, abide, till He should come. It may also reflect the hope of the brethren in that generation that He would come in their own time, and that hope may have been strengthened by their recollection of His cryptic words on another occasion: "Verily I say unto you, There be some standing here which shall not taste of death till they see the Son of Man coming in His kingdom" (Matt. 16: 28). Was there a link between this saying with regard to John and that other saying addressed to all the disciples?

YET JESUS SAID NOT UNTO HIM, HE SHALL NOT DIE: BUT, IF I WILL THAT HE TARRY TILL I COME, WHAT IS THAT TO THEE? These words correct the error or mistake by a simple repetition of what the Lord had said. This is done in a way which makes it clear that the error had not yet been disproved by fact. If this chapter had been written by the hand of another disciple some time after John's death, it would have been easy to dismiss the rumour by some record of the plain fact that he had died. But the cautious reserve in this comment implies that John was still alive and that he wrote these words with his own hand. He did not claim to know all that the Lord had meant; he was content to note what had been said. He did not read into that saying what others had tried to read; he would let time unfold the full meaning of God's purpose for him. There was a sense in which the Lord had come in the year of A.D. 70 when City and Temple were both destroyed, and he alone of the Twelve had lived to see that day and to take his place in the new economy. He still had to look out on the uncertainty of the future and dwell in the knowledge that his life was safe in the will of God. The Lord had not said that he would not die, nor did he fear the gate of death. But he had been called to tarry awhile, and this would make him quick to hear the last saying of all: "He which testifieth these things saith, Surely I come quickly." And the recollection of those words by the sea taught him the great *cri du coeur* in reply: "Amen. Even so, come, Lord Jesus" (Rev. 22: 20).

Peter and John who were so close to each other—like stars in a common orbit—were only to arrive at their final goal by separate paths of solitude. IF I WILL THAT HE TARRY TILL I COME, WHAT IS THAT TO THEE? What majesty, what deity, those words imply! He willed that the one, strong, eager, impetuous, a man of bold word and action, should spend years of faithful service and then lay down his life as a martyr: he was to bring hope and comfort to those who were called to face the fires of persecution, and how else could he have become the Apostle of suffering brethren? He willed that the other, loving, thoughtful, understanding, a man who was born for the skies, should live on when others had gone and die at last in great old age: he was to bear witness to the Living Lord and Saviour as the King and Judge of us all, and how else could he have fulfilled that task if he had not tarried till the Son of Man had come and Jerusalem had been destroyed? He knew which of the twain would be taken early and which would long abide: He ruled the path of each in love and it was not for one or the other to think that he could least be spared.[7] Therefore His summons to Peter carries equal weight for us all: FOLLOW THOU ME.

Chapter Seven

MANY OTHER THINGS

"This is the disciple which testifieth of these things and wrote these things: and we know that his testimony is true. And there are also many other things which Jesus did, the which if they should be written every one, I suppose that even the world itself could not contain the books that should be written. Amen."   JOHN 21: 24.25.

The two verses which bring St. John's Gospel to an end confront us with a literary problem: we are compelled to ask how they won their foothold in this chapter. Were they written by the same man who wrote the rest of the Gospel? And if not, was each verse written by the same hand or were there two distinct contributors? Plummer points out that the external evidence is in favour of the verdict that both verses should be ascribed to the same hand; and that this was the hand of the author of the final chapter; and that this was St. John himself.[1] No manuscript in existence lacks verse 24, and all but the Sinaitic and perhaps one cursive have verse 25 as well; and there is no evidence that there ever was a copy which lacked this last chapter and verse 24.[2] But it has been argued that the internal evidence all points to a different conclusion. The use of the plural in verse 24 (WE KNOW) is taken to suggest that this verse was added by the disciples of St. John at Ephesus, and the reversion to the singular in verse 25 (I SUPPOSE) is taken to suggest that this was a remark which the writer may have heard from St. John.[3] Westcott describes the two verses as "separate notes attached to the Gospel before its publication."[4] But such evidence is not conclusive and each verse needs separate discussion on its merits.

The first verse lays stress on the absolute veracity of the witness: THIS IS THE DISCIPLE WHICH TESTIFIETH OF THESE THINGS AND WROTE THESE THINGS: AND WE KNOW THAT HIS TESTIMONY IS TRUE. This verse is in a form which invites comparison with that of a similar verse at the close of the Passion narrative: "And he that saw it bare record, and his record is true: and he knoweth that he saith true that ye might believe" (John 19: 35). The third person in that verse is sustained throughout: "He that saw" is the same as the one of whom it is said that "he knoweth". But there is a transition in this verse from one who wrote in the third person to a voice in the first person: "The disciple which ... wrote these things" is in contrast with the phrase: "We know that his testimony is true." Perhaps the most natural impression which this creates is that others, independent of the Evangelist, were now adding their own word to confirm the truth of his record. Westcott takes this point of view on the ground that the pronoun must be treated as an honest plural and not as a literary device. Thus he argues that the verse may have been added by the Ephesian Elders who had received from him both the oral and the written contents of the Gospel; and in

this case, it served as a certificate for the authority of
the Gospel on its publication.[5]

But this verdict is not final, for to ascribe this verse to
an anonymous writer creates greater problems than
those which it resolves. There are others therefore who
still hold that it was written by the hand of St. John
himself as a final, solemn declaration of the authentic
character of his testimony. Surely if the Ephesian
Church had thought it wise or necessary to add such
an imprimatur, they would not have referred to the
veteran Apostle merely as "this disciple". It is true that
the phrase which speaks of the witness as still present[6]
does not prove that John was alive when this note was
written;[7] but that is the natural inference, and it is in
harmony with the narrative. But there would have
been no need for others to add such a confirmation
while he was still alive: and if they had done so after
his death, would it have been left in this form? The
Lord's saying that John was to tarry had prompted the
rumour that he would not see death: and if in fact he
were now dead, would such a verse as this leave that
rumour on record without a comment?

We have to wait until we reach this verse in the
Gospel to learn that its author was "the disciple whom
Jesus loved" (John 21: 20), and this phrase in the third
person, THIS IS THE DISCIPLE, was quite in keeping with
the anonymous humility which was sustained from first
to last. The phrase, WE KNOW, was not inconsistent with
this anonymous form of self-reference. Bishop Moule
points out that he loved to put himself aside and to
speak AB EXTRA as it were of himself.[8] Perhaps he was
about to close this last chapter of his Gospel when he

resolved to associate with himself his most intimate disciples as those who could confirm its truth. With a glance of confident affection round the group to which he had so often told the story by word of mouth, he would join them all with himself in this final testimony to the truth of THESE THINGS.[9] Such a term might refer only to the contents of this final chapter, but it is more likely that it takes in the whole Gospel (cf. John 20: 31). The phrase WE KNOW would have been out of place when he spoke of details which he had seen with his own eyes at the foot of the Cross; for that, he was bound to say "he knoweth" (John 19: 35). But "he knoweth" might well become WE KNOW as he allowed others to share with him in joint witness to the veracity of his record.

The next verse lays stress on the infinite variety of the Gospel: AND THERE ARE ALSO MANY OTHER THINGS WHICH JESUS DID, THE WHICH, IF THEY SHOULD BE WRITTEN EVERY ONE, I SUPPOSE THAT EVEN THE WORLD ITSELF COULD NOT CONTAIN THE BOOKS THAT SHOULD BE WRITTEN. This last fervent declaration marks a fresh change in the subject of the sentence and is in a style and language which in certain respects are quite unlike those of St. John. The phrase, WE KNOW, which had involved a change both in person and in number, now becomes I SUPPOSE, with a change in number but not person. This seems to indicate a change in authorship; but who is meant? Plummer notes that it was unlike St. John to write in the first person at all unless in the plural number and he thought that its use was a sign that the verse had been added by a fresh hand. This

might have been the case if the writer were anxious to
perserve something which he had heard John say, and
the wording seems to imply that the recollection of
those things was still fresh. Material was not only
available; it was abundant in the form of oral tradition:
and it would still have been easy to commit to writing
what ear and eye witnesses were able to contribute.[10]

Lightfoot believed that this verse was written either
by St. John or by one of his intimate disciples. It seemed
evident to him that it was meant as a scholium, a
comment or footnote at the end of the text of the
Gospel. He was impressed by Tischendorf's discovery
that in the Sinaitic manuscript it appears in hand
writing different from that in the rest of the text. He
was also interested in the fact that one valuable cursive
(63) appears at first sight to omit the verse altogether,
for the last page ends with the words of verse 24 as
though the scribe had come to the end of his text.
But a careful study of both the text and its scholia points
to the fact that the manuscript has lost a leaf, and that
when that leaf was in place it must have contained
verse 25. And since this verse is found in all other
extant copies, and these come from many varied sources,
we may safely infer that it records St. John's own words
(cf. John 20: 30) and that it was written either by him
or by one of his friends.[11]

There were "many other signs" which the Lord Jesus
had wrought in the presence of His disciples (John
20: 30); there were MANY OTHER THINGS which He had
done but which have no written record. He had never
wasted time or strength in idle words or actions while
here on earth, and this very Gospel is at most only a

brief and beautiful selection of all that He began both
to do and to teach. A world full of books could not have
told the story in full; all the letters of the alphabet
could not fully portray Him Who is both Alpha and
Omega. This bold hyperbole that the whole world
could not contain the books which might have been
written does no more than reflect the deep yearning of
His disciples down the centuries. We have received no
more than a fragment of His earthly record, and that
fragment is as fresh and vital now as ever. What more
would be required to fill out that fragment to the
utmost? How much would be needed to complete the
record of the MANY OTHER THINGS which He did?[12]
And yet if men do not believe what is written, neither
would they believe even in a world full of books about
the Son of God.

St. John outlived all "the brethren", and like the last
swallow that lingers when others have gone, he still
remained when they had sought summer in climes
above. In the mellow evening of his life at Ephesus,
those great days of the Son of Man would live again
in his memory. They would dawn once more in his
mind like a dream of heaven; they had indeed been
like days of heaven on earth. There were days in Galilee
when he had seen His glory; and that summer day
down by the river Jordan when he had heard words full
of grace and truth; and those forty days before Olivet
when he had drunk from the wells of the Kingdom. All
the "many other things" which Jesus did were still in
his heart, and his conversation was all absorbed in the
life and work of Emmanuel. He would confide to his

disciples what there had not been room to relate in his narrative and so would make them trustees of this unwritten Evangel. And who were they? Polycarp sat at his feet as he had sat at the feet of Jesus; Irenaeus would one day sit at the feet of Polycarp as he had sat at the feet of St. John. They treasured his testimony as true, and they knew that the world itself could not contain all the books that might be written to declare His glory. AMEN.[13]

Chapter Eight

I AM WITH YOU

"And lo, I am with you alway, even unto the end
of the world. Amen."   MATT. 28:20

The Lord's encounter with His disciples by the Sea of
Galilee was followed by another appearance which is
described only in St. Matthew's Gospel. The scene was
in those hills which stand like a girdle round the waters
beneath and the disciples had gone there by appoint-
ment for a further meeting. They had been told that
they would see Him in that hill country and they had
left Jerusalem with that object in view: "Then the
eleven disciples went away into Galilee into a mountain
where Jesus had appointed them" (Matt. 28: 16).
Perhaps they were not there alone; this may have been
the great moment when "He was seen of above five
hundred brethren at once" (1 Cor. 15: 6). They came
full of eager expectation, and yet they were taken by
glad surprise: "And when they saw Him they worshipped Him: but some doubted" (Matt. 28: 17). Their
first sight of Him may have been on the rim of a hill
at a distance (cf. John 21: 4), and some doubted
whether it were the Lord until they saw Him near at
hand. But all doubt would vanish when He "came"
and began to speak (Matt. 28: 18). He would speak in
the quiet tones of ordinary conversation, but His words

were full of boundless magnificence.[1] He Who had
once refused all the kingdoms of the world in return
for a moment's homage to the Tempter had now
received supreme authority both in heaven and earth.
He was once more in those hills where He had chosen
the twelve that they might be with Him and that He
might send them forth to proclaim His word (Mark
3: 13.14): now they were to go and establish disciples[2]
in all nations by baptism and instruction, and He
would be with them right on to the end of the world.

These words refer to the spiritual reality of His
presence with men: AND LO, I AM WITH YOU ALWAY,
EVEN UNTO THE END OF THE WORLD. It is remarkable
how each of the Evangelists records a distinct and
decisive utterance by the risen Saviour on the future
proclamation of the Gospel. Thus St. Matthew records
how He gave the disciples His great commission: "Go
ye therefore and teach all nations, baptizing them in
the Name of the Father and of the Son and of the
Holy Ghost" (Matt. 28: 19). St. Mark includes among
His last sayings the words: "Go ye into all the world
and preach the Gospel to every creature" (Mark 16: 15).
St. Luke relates how He declared "that repentance and
remission of sins should be preached in His Name
among all nations" (Luke 24: 47). St. John preserves
the charge that was most characteristic of his Gospel:
"As my Father hath sent Me, even so send I you"
(John 20: 21). And to these four sayings must be added
the words preserved by St. Luke in The Acts: "Ye shall
be witnesses unto Me ... unto the uttermost part of
the earth" (Acts 1: 8). Thus the first great task for that

band of men was to make Christ known to "every
creature", "in all the world", "among all nations",
"unto the uttermost part of the earth". But the Lord
knew all too well that men are quick to complain if
their leaders do not march at their head or take the
field with them. Therefore lest the command GO YE
should seem too hard, He went on at once to add the
words of promise: AND LO, I AM WITH YOU ALWAY.
That would set all things right, for it told them that
those who go where He would have them go will have
Him with them wherever they go.

AND LO, I AM WITH YOU ALWAY: This is something
which transcends all human limitations, for it is God's
presence with man. Those who go at His call are not
unmindful of the severance of their home ties: they
leave behind those whom they love; they face untried
paths of personal loneliness. Our hearts may go with
them, and we strive to follow them with our prayers;
but they are no longer with us, and we are no longer
with them. Yet they are not alone, for His Name is
Emmanuel: God is with us; He is with them (Matt.
1:23). This helps us at once to understand the real
character of this promise: the Lord was not speaking
of His presence in the body; He spoke of His presence
by means of His Spirit in the hearts of those who serve
Him. Only six days before His death, He had told the
Twelve in plainest language: "The poor always ye have
with you; but Me ye have not always" (John 12:8).
And on the night on which He was betrayed, He had
spoken freely of the "little while" that He would still
be with them (John 13:33; 14:19), and of the fact
that He was soon to "go away" (John 14:2; 16:5).

Death would remove Him from their midst and His presence in the body would be withdrawn. But He would not leave them in this world as orphans, nor would He send them out alone. He could only be present in body in one place at one time, but there are no limitations to His presence by means of His Spirit where two or three meet in His Name (Matt. 18: 20). Thus the warning on the eve of the Cross, ME YE HAVE NOT ALWAYS, was more than matched by this promise after He rose again: I AM WITH YOU ALWAY; for He will be with His people to the end of time in all that speaks of spiritual reality.

God had often assured the heart of this man or that man that He would be with him; no true servant of His had been without kindred words of comfort. Jacob as a fugitive from his family, asleep in the desert, a stone for his pillow, the sky for his ceiling, saw the ladder between earth and heaven and heard God say: "I am with thee" (Gen. 28: 15). Moses as an exile from the court of Egypt, at the back-side of the desert, saw that strange sight, the bush that burned and yet was not consumed, and heard God say: "I will be with thee" (Exod. 3: 12). David as a warrior on the hills of Bethlehem, where he had watched his sheep, and fought with the lion and the bear, feared no evil, for he could say: "Thou art with me" (Ps. 23: 4). Moses indeed had felt after the failure of Israel while he was in the Mount that he could not go on unless God were to go with him, and the promise had been renewed with the glorious assurance: "My presence shall go with thee, and I will give thee rest" (Exod. 33: 14). That great promise to Jacob and Moses had been the strength and stay of

God's servants in many a crisis,[3] and it was a well-known fact that God had been as good as His word. But now every promise of old was caught up with sovereign finality in the words of the Lord Jesus: AND LO, I AM WITH YOU ALWAY. There is something both sweet and grand in that one word, ALWAY: it stretches into the future and it reaches to the ends of the earth; it transcends all boundaries of time and all horizons of need. The God Who has been with us in the past and Who is with us here and now is the God Who will be with us ALWAY as the future unfolds and the consummation of the ages draws near at last.

These words also refer to the continuing reality of His presence with men: AND LO, I AM WITH YOU ALWAY, EVEN UNTO THE END OF THE WORLD. The Lord Jesus would soon ascend from their midst and return to that glory which had been His before the worlds were made. He would be lost to sight once He had passed beyond the skies and would be seen of men no more until He rends the veil to come again. They were henceforth to walk by faith and not by sight, but they were not deprived of the strength and comfort of His presence. He would have them know that He is still the Eternal Companion of all who bear His Name; He is always visible to the eye of faith, tangible to the touch of love. That great promise was not confined to the first disciples or the first century; it was meant for all the redeemed in each generation until He comes again. The quiet language of our English Version hides the technical character of the phrase: THE END OF THE WORLD. It is used no less than five times in St. Matthew's

Gospel,[4] and it should be rendered: THE CONSUMMATION OF THE AGE (R.V.M.). It was derived from Jewish apocalyptic literature which thought of the present age as the last in a series of ages, and as itself drawing to its end or consummation.[5] And this promise declares that His presence with His people is a continuing reality till that end comes and that new age begins. He is more than mortal man or angel being, and He will be with us each day and all the days until His own return in power and great glory.

EVEN UNTO THE END OF THE WORLD: This is a word on which we can rely to the utmost limit of need and time. It is like a block of granite beneath our feet, and it will stand firm through all the vicissitudes of life. We live in a world that is full of change, and few things long remain the same; but there is one changeless Friend and Master, and His word will not pass away. He Who died on the cross and Who rose from the grave after the power of an endless life is the same yesterday and today and for ever. He will not disappoint our faith, for this promise has never been recalled; He will neither fail nor forsake those who trust Him, for His presence has never been withdrawn. "Thus saith the Lord that created thee O Jacob, and He that formed thee O Israel: Fear not, for I have redeemed thee; I have called thee by thy name; thou art Mine: when though passest through the waters, I WILL BE WITH THEE; and through the rivers, they shall not overflow thee" (Isa. 43: 1.2). And He is as truly with His servants now as He was that day when He stood in their midst on the hills above the Sea and spoke the words that look far on to the end of the age.

Those words of the mighty Victor over death and the grave are the herald of the final triumph of the Gospel. The day when the kingdoms of this world shall be the kingdom of our God and His Son must have appeared infinitely remote to this band of wondering disciples; but if God be for us, who can prevail against the least of us? When the modern missionary movement first came into being with the foundation of the various societies at the close of the eighteenth century, the great compelling motive of the early missionaries was that of compassion for a world that was lost. Men like Carey and Martyn and Judson never ceased to hear the thud of Christless feet that trod the path to eternity. Perhaps today the great motive is that of obedience to the command to go into all the world and preach the Gospel in the hearing of all mankind. This once found a slogan in the call to "evangelize to a finish and to bring back the King". But whichever is uppermost as a motive, the need could not be more urgent. And vast as is the task to bring the world to the feet of Jesus, there is no need to fear failure; for all authority both in heaven and earth belongs to Him, and He will be with us until this age comes to an end. When John Wesley's life moved towards its close in March 1791, he took his leave of those who were in the room by lifting up his arm and saying with a triumph that cannot be expressed: "The best of all is, God is with us."[6] That is the grand secret of all that has ever been done for the Kingdom of God, for to have Him with us means more than to have ten thousand armies at our command.

This was David Livingstone's text. One hot summer

night in January 1856, he found himself hemmed in by
a cordon of savage and hostile tribesmen. Sixteen years
he had spent in Africa, and he had never been in such
peril before. For the first time in all those years, he felt
tempted to steal away and seek safety in flight under
the cover of darkness. But he laid his finger once more
on these words of promise in his Bible: AND LO, I AM
WITH YOU ALWAY, EVEN UNTO THE END OF THE WORLD.
Those words were copied out in his Journal and were
scored by his pen. Then he went on to say: "It is the
word of a Gentleman of the most strict and sacred
honour, so there's an end of it. I will not cross furtively
tonight as I intended . . . I feel quite calm now, thank
God." Later in the same year, he went home to Scot-
land. When at length he announced his resolve to
return, a great hush fell on his hearers as he told them
how he would go back in the strength of that promise:
"for", he said, "on those words I staked everything, and
they never failed."[7] This great promise ends with one
word in the English Version: AMEN. That word does
not belong to the Greek text; it may have been added
in course of time as a word of heart-felt assent. As for
ourselves, can we lift up our eyes and look without fear
in His face? Can we hear that golden word of promise,
and then like that nameless scribe add our glad AMEN:
So be it, Lord!

Chapter Nine

CARRIED UP INTO HEAVEN

"And He led them out as far as to Bethany, and He
lifted up His hands, and blessed them. And it came
to pass while He blessed them, He was parted from
them and carried up into heaven."

LUKE 24: 50.51.

St. Luke is the only Evangelist who attempts to describe
the Ascension from Olivet, and he records it both in his
Gospel and in The Acts as the last scene in the visible
ministry of Christ on earth. Forty days had elapsed
since He had burst the bands of death to rise again;
they had been days in which "He shewed Himself
alive" among His own both in Judaea and in Galilee
(Acts 1: 3). He had furnished many proofs of His great
resurrection, and He had taught His last lesson in things
that had to do with God's Kingdom. He had appeared
to them from time to time at will; He had vanished
before their eyes and gone they knew not where. His
exaltation had begun and the time was at hand for the
last scene of all. The series of visitations was thus brought
to an end with this unique event and the character of
the Ascension marked it out as final. AND HE LED THEM
OUT AS FAR AS TO BETHANY, AND HE LIFTED UP HIS HANDS,
AND BLESSED THEM: AND IT CAME TO PASS WHILE HE
BLESSED THEM, HE WAS PARTED FROM THEM, AND CARRIED
UP INTO HEAVEN. The Acts repeats this in substance,

leaving out one or two details, adding others which complete the picture: "And when He had spoken these things, while they beheld, He was taken up, and a cloud received Him out of their sight" (Acts 1: 9). There is only one verse in the other Gospels which speaks of this event at all, and it reads more like a credal statement than a factual narrative. But it bears out St. Luke's two-fold account and is valuable testimony to the event itself: "So then after the Lord had spoken unto them, He was received up into heaven, and sat on the right hand of God" (Mark 16: 19).

The last interview with the disciples must have been in or near Jerusalem; they had travelled south from Galilee and had assembled in the city where He met them: AND HE LED THEM OUT AS FAR AS TO BETHANY, AND HE LIFTED UP HIS HANDS, AND BLESSED THEM. Perhaps He had met them once more in that upper room where they had met on the eve of His Passion (Luke 22: 12), and the conversation now as then was carried on as He led them out of the city, across the brook Kidron, towards the Mount of Olives. He did not pause now as before at the Garden; He led them on towards the fold in the hills which held a peaceful village. "He led them out until they were over against Bethany" (R.V.); that is, until they could look in the direction of Bethany. The words may be interpreted by the subsequent reference to the return of the disciples: "Then returned they unto Jerusalem from the mount called Olivet which is from Jerusalem a sabbath day's journey" (Acts 1: 12). This would be five or six furlongs from the city and points to a place in the hills about half-way between Jerusalem and Bethany. It must have been reasonably remote from each, and yet within sight of the quiet village towards which they could look.[1] This journey was unique, for it was the only time after the resurrection that He led them as of old from one place to another.[2] It may remind us of the last journey of Elijah with Elisha before he was caught up before the young man's eyes: but did these men know as he knew that God would take away their Head that day? (2 Kings 2: 3). He had foretold it on the eve of His Passion: "I go to prepare a place for you . . . and whither I go ye know" (John 14: 2.4). He had told them before it came to pass so that when His words were fulfilled, they might believe (John 14: 29). He had confirmed it to Mary on the resurrection morning: "I ascend unto My Father and your Father, and to My God and your God" (John 20: 17). If the disciples understood as Elisha had understood, did they cry out like him for a double portion of their Master's Spirit?

AND HE LED THEM OUT AS FAR AS TO BETHANY: As they trod the winding path that led them to the Mount of Olives, His last words were spoken. St. Luke in his Gospel draws a veil of silence over that last conversation, but its fragments have been preserved in three verses in his other version of this event (Acts 1: 6.8). It all arose from a question which they ventured to ask as they followed the road: "Lord, wilt Thou at this time restore again the kingdom to Israel?" (Acts 1: 6). It was the old question which they had so often discussed (cf. Luke 24: 21), and it shows how they clung to their hopes for material splendour. They had no doubt at all that He was The Christ to Whom the Prophets had borne witness, but they still thought that The Christ would in due time set up an earthly throne in Jerusalem. They could not grasp the fact that His kingdom was not like an earthly kingdom and they were sure that He meant to restore its glory to Israel. The Lord did not comment again on this mistaken conception; He was content in His reply to lay down the narrow limits of all human knowledge: "It is not for you to know the times or the seasons which the Father hath put in His own power" (Acts 1: 7). Then He went on to speak of the wide field that stretched before them in service for Him: "But ye shall receive power after that the Holy Ghost is come upon you: and ye shall be witnesses unto Me both in Jerusalem, and in all Judaea, and in Samaria, and unto the uttermost part of the earth" (Acts 1: 8). This was like a compass which would open out from Jerusalem as its centre to the ends of the earth, and their task will not be complete until the ends of the earth are possessed for Him.

AND HE LIFTED UP HIS HANDS, AND BLESSED THEM: That great saying was still fresh in their minds when they came to a halt up in the hills. They stood in a little group round the Lord and He lifted up His hands to bless them. Both His action and His blessing would make it plain that this was a final farewell, and great tenderness breathes its softening calm through it all. It was as though He would focus their eyes upon His hands as they were raised, for they would see the prints where they had been pierced and nailed to the cross. They were the visible scars of His atoning death; they were the permanent seals of His redeeming love.

They were the marks of His continuing identity; they were the proofs of His resurrection reality. His first action when He had first stood in their midst was to show them His hands (Luke 24: 40); and now His last action when He was to leave them was to lift up those hands. We can easily imagine how that little band of men would look and listen; He had not dealt with them like this before, and their eyes would shine with wonder. Jacob and Esau had struggled to obtain the blessing of their father Isaac; Jacob and Moses had striven to pronounce a blessing on the tribes of Israel. But such blessings could not compare with the benediction of the risen Saviour. Bishop Ryle says that He had come to bless and not to curse, and blessing He would go away; He had come in mercy and not in wrath, and in mercy He would return to His Father.[3] We are not told in what words that benediction was phrased, but this was the blessing that makes men rich and that has no sorrow in it at all (Prov. 10: 22).

It was while His hands were still rasied in the act of blessing that He began to ascend in glory: AND IT CAME TO PASS WHILE HE BLESSED THEM, HE WAS PARTED FROM THEM AND CARRIED UP INTO HEAVEN. The last look and the last words of those whom we love are for ever engraved on the tablets of mind and heart: and so it must have been for those who stood beneath those upraised hands. For how would the parting take place? It would be while in the very act of blessing. There was a sense in which the Lord had been eager for His Passion; it had been with "desire" that He had faced the Cross (Luke 22: 15). But He had been in no haste to ascend; He waited forty days, and then He was separated from them. There was exquisite gentleness in this as a final demonstration of His loving kindness for them, for it was a slow and deliberate movement, carried out with calm and impressive majesty. These men who had followed Him for three years on the hot and dusty highways had to remain behind; therefore He went away in a manner that would cheer their faith and brace their courage when He had gone. He did not part from them until the last word of blessing had been calmly spoken; then He withdrew as the unseen arm of God took Him up before their eyes.

HE WAS PARTED FROM THEM AND CARRIED UP INTO HEAVEN: Brief but beautiful is this description of His ascent into glory, and more details are supplied from elsewhere. The last phrase, that He was CARRIED UP, borne aloft, does not appear in some important manuscripts; but there is no dispute about the text when we turn to The Acts, and this makes it clear that He was TAKEN UP, caught away. St. Luke also twice makes use of another expression which is rendered "taken up" in the A.V. and "received up" in the R.V. (Acts 1:2,11); but this seems to describe the whole movement rather than its process. Thus He PARTED from them and was TAKEN UP by the hand of God; and they watched Him as He WENT on His way (Acts 1:10) until He was RECEIVED UP out of sight (Acts 1:11). It was neither like the ascent of Enoch nor the rapture of Elijah; there was neither violent hurricane nor fiery chariot to lift Him up or to bear Him away. Nor was it like the way in which He had vanished before men's eyes when He had been seated with them at the table (Luke

24: 31): for now He went up in full view with great glory until He passed beyond their sight.

HE WAS PARTED FROM THEM AND CARRIED UP INTO HEAVEN: They watched Him go until "a cloud received Him out of their sight" (Acts 1 : 9). Once the winter has passed, the skies over Jerusalem are cloudless and sun-lit for months on end; the most ordinary cloud at the end of spring would be sufficiently conspicuous. And yet it is far from certain whether any eyes saw that cloud on the Mount of Olives except the eyes of those who watched Him go. It was like that special cloud which had been seen to overshadow Him when He was transfigured on "the holy mount" in full view of three disciples (2 Pet. 1: 18; Luke 9: 34). Such a cloud had once been the sign of God's presence with His people: it was ordained to rest on the tabernacle as a token of the glory that dwelt within (Exod. 40: 34). It was reminiscent also of the prophetic description of His coming again: "Then shall they see the Son of Man coming in a cloud with power and great glory" (Luke 21: 27). So now a cloud received the Lord in His resurrection body where no eye could follow. But though He passed beyond their sight, He would ascend in glory to glory, and it is from a great Messianic Psalm of David that we now fill out the picture. Mortal eyes could not see the great host of angels or the golden gates of glory, nor could mortal ears hear the great shout of triumph from the angel convoy: "Lift up your heads, O ye gates; and be ye lift up, ye everlasting doors; and the King of glory shall come in" (Ps. 24: 7). And thus He "passed through the heavens" (Heb. 4: 14 R.V.), "far above all" (Eph. 4: 10), and "sat down

G

on the right hand of the Majesty on high" (Heb. 1: 3).
"We see Jesus Who was made a little lower than the
angels for the suffering of death crowned with glory
and honour" (Heb. 2: 9).

The Ascension from Olivet and the coronation at
God's right hand were the final stages in the exaltation
of the Risen Saviour: "Wherefore also God highly
exalted Him and gave Him the Name which is above
every name: that in the Name of Jesus every knee
should bow . . . and that every tongue should confess
that Jesus Christ is Lord" (Phil. 2: 9.11 R.V.). But that
was all beyond human seeing; the last sight that mortal
eyes were allowed was as He went up in a trail of glory.
St. Luke's account of the disciples who stood gazing
upward as He was swept beyond their sight may have
prompted Tennyson's description of Sir Bedivere who
strained his eyes to watch the barge which bore the
sore wounded Arthur to his last bourne. And as he
gazed, there came to him across the lake, faint and far
off as from the edge of time, sounds of triumph and joy:

> "Sounds, as if some fair city were one voice
> Around a king returning from his wars".[4]

It is enough to lift our thoughts to that shout of triumph
which went rolling among the stars when the King of
glory went in; it was as if the fair city of God were then
one voice around her King as He returned from all
His wars (Isa. 63: 1).

Chapter Ten

THIS SAME JESUS

"And while they looked stedfastly toward heaven as He went up, behold, two men stood by them in white apparel; which also said, Ye men of Galilee, why stand ye gazing up into Heaven? This same Jesus which is taken up from you into heaven shall so come in like manner as ye have seen Him go into heaven. Then returned they unto Jerusalem from the mount called Olivet, which is from Jerusalem a sabbath day's journey."

ACTS I : 10.12.

The disciples on Olivet stood in silent awe and wonder, lost in artless desire to pierce beyond the cloud which had received Him out of sight. Such an upward gaze, long after gazing had grown useless, was in accord with all human nature: it is just so that men gaze out to sea, fixing their eyes on the spot where they last saw the ship that bears a loved one away. How long they stood and gazed we are not told; perhaps they hoped that the cloud would dissolve as once before and leave Him in their midst (cf. Matt. 17: 5.8). Such a hope was in vain, but their stedfast upward gaze brought its own reward: AND WHILE THEY LOOKED STEDFASTLY TOWARD HEAVEN AS HE WENT UP, BEHOLD, TWO MEN STOOD BY THEM IN WHITE APPAREL. St. Luke plainly means that these were angels who had returned from the escort beyond the cloud to greet and guide them with words of hope and comfort. There is remarkable economy in the Gospel records with regard to angels, but these TWO MEN . . . IN WHITE APPAREL on the Mount of Olives correspond with the "two men . . . in shining garments" by the tomb of Joseph (Luke 24: 4). Their blunt question, WHY STAND YE GAZING UP INTO HEAVEN? was in the same manner as that on the Resurrection morning: "Why seek ye the living among the dead?" (Luke 24: 5). And the reason which they supplied, THIS SAME JESUS . . . SHALL SO COME IN LIKE MANNER AS YE HAVE SEEN HIM GO, was not dissimilar from the reason which they furnished on the earlier occasion: "He is not here, but is risen" (Luke 24: 6). Such words told them plainly that this separation was both final, and not final: it was final in the sense that they would know Him no more after the flesh, yet it was not final in the sense that He would return at length with great glory in like manner as they had seen Him go.

These words lay strong emphasis in the first place on the fact of His final return: THIS SAME JESUS WHICH IS TAKEN UP FROM YOU INTO HEAVEN SHALL COME. The name JESUS was the name which had been disclosed by the angel before His birth: "Thou shalt call His name Jesus, for He shall save His people from their sins" (Matt. 1: 21). It was a name which had declared His humanity and humility, the name by which He was known while He trod this earth as Man with men. It was JESUS Who had loved "to the end" (John 13: 1) and had died on the Cross: it was THIS SAME JESUS Who had burst from the grave and had stood "in the midst"

(John 20: 19). His Ascent in glory from the Mount of Olives was the sign that God would exalt His name above all names, and the men who had known Him as JESUS were henceforth to confess Him as the Lord (Phil. 2: 9.11). The change is marked as the text of The Acts unfolds, and the bare name JESUS becomes THE LORD JESUS (cf. Acts 1 : 21). This change was made clear in the magnificent peroration of Peter's address ten days later: "Therefore let all the house of Israel know assuredly that God hath made that same Jesus Whom ye have crucified both Lord and Christ" (Acts 2: 36). The words of the angels after the Ascension from Olivet mark the dividing-line between the old and the new with regard to the use of this name and have special significance on this account alone. THIS SAME JESUS Whom they had seen alive with the print of the nails in hands and feet would come again: He had not lost His reality in the interval between death and resurrection, nor would He lose His identity in the interval between His going away and coming again.

This emphasis is amplified by the reference to His Ascension on high: THIS SAME JESUS WHICH IS TAKEN UP FROM YOU INTO HEAVEN SHALL COME. The whole scene was mysterious from the common view-point of men, and the element of mystery was still further increased by the atmosphere of majesty. These disciples from Galilee must have fallen under its spell as they sensed the sublime, but they had no intuitive explanation of what they saw until they heard the words of the angels. He had withdrawn from their midst with surprising suddenness on the earlier occasions; that would perhaps make them marvel the more at this calm, slow ascent before their eyes. But the angels made it clear what this meant: He was TAKEN UP . . . INTO HEAVEN. They had seen Him TAKEN UP in bodily majesty against all the ordinary laws of nature or the experience of men. They had seen Him slowly ascend until that cloud concealed Him in its folds and He vanished beyond their sight. There was no room for doubt, for they could not deny what they had seen. And the angels would help them to perceive that He had now "passed out of the present sphere of being into one which is beyond the furthest limits which we can conceive".[1] It would take time before they could readily interpret what their eyes had seen or their ears had heard, and it remained for St. Paul to give it classical expression: "He that descended is the same also that ascended up far above all heavens that He might fill all things" (Eph. 4: 10).

But their wistful gaze up into heaven was met by this promise: THIS SAME JESUS WHICH IS TAKEN UP FROM YOU INTO HEAVEN SHALL COME. The Lord Himself during the night on which He was betrayed had given them the same assurance: "In My Father's house are many mansions: if it were not so, I would have told you. I go to prepare a place for you. And if I go and prepare a place for you, I will come again and receive you unto Myself, that where I am, there ye may be also" (John 14: 2.3). And this consolation was now renewed by the angels in terms full of kindness. They did not say that we shall go to Him; they said that He will come to us. He has passed out of sight until earth and time reach the end: then the gates will once more lift up their heads and the King of glory will return in triumph.

THIS SAME JESUS . . . SHALL COME; He will descend even
as they saw Him ascend. And the vision of this final
event has been the hope and strength of the Church
through all the ages of its struggle with the hosts of
darkness. Experience has proved that when this hope
has been firmly embraced, it can lift and control human
life with a strength which no other motive is able to
exert.[2] "We know that when He shall appear, we shall
be like Him, for we shall see Him as He is: and every
man that hath this hope in Him purifieth himself even
as He is pure" (1 John 3: 2.3).

These words lay strong emphasis in the next place
on the mode of His return: THIS SAME JESUS . . . SHALL
SO COME IN LIKE MANNER AS YE HAVE SEEN HIM GO INTO
HEAVEN. This is the most precise statement in the New
Testament on the nature of His Return, and it declares
that its detail will be similar to that of His departure.
He will come again in Person; it is THIS SAME JESUS, not
some other person, for Whom we are to look. This is
something totally different from the visitation of grace
for the Church on the day of Pentecost or the visitation
of wrath for the Jews at the fall of Jerusalem; the only
true analogy is the Incarnation which took place at
His first advent in the manger at Bethlehem. Did He
ascend in body? Then in body He will return, and not
as a spirit. Did they behold His Person? Then in person
He will return, and not as a phantom. He will come
again in glory; it is IN LIKE MANNER that He will come,
and the glory of His Return will be tenfold. It will be
in mighty contrast with His advent before when He
came down in lowliness and poverty, and in the meek-

ness of childhood. It will be in glorious harmony with His exaltation when He went up in confidence and majesty, and in the splendour of Godhead. "The Lord Jesus shall be revealed from heaven with His mighty angels . . . when He shall come to be glorified in His saints and to be admired in all them that believe" (2 Thess. 1: 7.10).

This emphasis is amplified by the reference to His Ascension on high: THIS SAME JESUS . . . SHALL SO COME IN LIKE MANNER AS YE HAVE SEEN HIM GO INTO HEAVEN. While they yet stood and watched, they saw divine symbols of His glory, and those symbols will be the marks of His Return. The first symbol was the cloud which received Him out of sight, and there will be trailing clouds of glory at His coming again. He had Himself foretold this fact on two separate occasions. In His discourse on the Mount of Olives, He had declared: "And they shall see the Son of Man coming in the clouds of heaven with power and great glory" (Matt. 24: 30). In His statement on oath in the court of judgement, He had declared again: "Hereafter shall ye see the Son of Man sitting on the right hand of power and coming in the clouds of heaven" (Matt. 26: 64). St. Paul was to impress this fact on his readers: "We which are alive and remain shall be caught up . . . in the clouds to meet the Lord in the air" (1 Thess. 4: 17). St. John also was to recall it with picturesque emphasis: "Behold, He cometh with clouds, and every eye shall see Him" (Rev. 1: 7). And the other symbol of which they were conscious was the presence of the angels, and there will be mighty hosts of angels at His coming again. He had also foretold this fact on two separate occasions. In his conversation at Caesarea Philippi, He had declared: "The Son of Man shall come in the glory of His Father with His angels" (Matt. 16: 27). In His discourse on the Mount of Olives, He had again declared: "The Son of Man shall come in His glory, and all the holy angels with Him" (Matt. 25: 31). Had an angel host in the skies of Bethlehem proclaimed His first Advent, and will not all the angels of God in the skies of glory unite to proclaim His Return?

Thus their earnest gaze up into heaven was met by this promise: THIS SAME JESUS . . . SHALL SO COME IN LIKE MANNER AS YE HAVE SEEN HIM GO INTO HEAVEN. The two angels made no attempt to say when this would be; and that, for the best of reasons. The Lord Himself had made it clear that "of that day and hour knoweth no man, no, not the angels of heaven" (Matt. 24: 36). The Scriptures are silent as to the time of His coming, and men recklessly speculate in vain. These same disciples on this same mount had once tried to elicit a great deal more in the way of detail: "Tell us," they said, "when shall these things be, and what shall be the sign of Thy coming?" (Matt. 24: 3). But it was not for them to know the time which God has kept in His own power (Acts 1: 7). He had drawn an illustration from the Old Testament to convey the effect which His coming will have on the world as a whole: "As the days of Noah were, so shall also the coming of the Son of Man be" (Matt. 24: 37). It will startle the whole careless, indifferent, unexpecting society of men who are immersed in their worldly affairs as though there will never be a day of judgement. The New Testament prophecies make use of three dramatic metaphors to

indicate the suddenness of this event: it will come like
a thief in the night (1 Thess. 5: 2; 2 Pet. 3: 10), in the
twinkling of an eye (1 Cor. 15: 52), and like a flash of
lightning (Matt. 24: 27). So shall it be when the Son of
Man comes again in His own and in His Father's
glory, with the angels of God as His escort and the
clouds of heaven as "the dust of His feet "(Nahum 1: 3).

The disciples on Olivet were like new men in a new
world when they had heard these things. They could
turn from that long upward gaze to face the future
with a sense of glorious certainty. THEN RETURNED THEY
UNTO JERUSALEM FROM THE MOUNT CALLED OLIVET
WHICH IS FROM JERUSALEM A SABBATH DAY'S JOURNEY.
St. Luke adds one or two details in his Gospel: "And
they worshipped Him, and returned to Jerusalem with
great joy" (Luke 24: 52). There they would be in the
midst of men who had put Him to death on the Cross,
but they were unafraid. They "were continually in the
temple, praising and blessing God" (Luke 24: 53). The
Lord had told them on the eve of His Passion that they
would have sorrow, but that He would turn their sorrow
to joy: "I will see you again, and your heart shall
rejoice" (John 16: 22). And so had it all come to pass;
they had been "glad when they saw the Lord" (John
20: 20). Theirs was joy which no man could take from
them even when they saw Him ascend and knew that
they would see Him as of old no more. They could only
praise and bless God, for theirs was the promise that
time could not dim nor death take away. They had seen
Him go in cloud and glory; in cloud and glory He will
come again.[3]

THE HOLY SPIRIT

John the Baptist was "filled with the Holy Ghost even from his mother's womb" (Luke 1: 15), and he entered upon his ministry "in the spirit and power of Elijah" (Luke 1: 17). But his mission was that of a herald; he was sent to prepare the way for the One that should come. All four Gospels record his plain declaration that a greater than he was to appear and that this was the One Who would baptize with the Holy Ghost (Matt. 3: 11; Mark 1: 8; Luke 3: 16; John 1: 33). They all record that when He did appear and was Himself baptized in the river Jordan, the Holy Ghost came upon Him and abode with Him (Matt. 3: 16; Mark 1: 10; Luke 3: 22; John 1: 32). St. John was to declare that "God giveth not the Spirit by measure unto Him" (John 3: 34), and that "Him hath God the Father sealed" (John 6: 27). All the Gospels supply abundant evidence of the reality and truth of such statements. Thus after His baptism, we read that "Jesus being full of the Holy Ghost returned from Jordan and was led by the Spirit into the wilderness" (Luke 4: 1). After the ordeal of temptation, "Jesus returned in the power of the Spirit into Galilee" (Luke 4: 14). When He came to Nazareth and sat in the synagogue, the passage of Scripture which He read and which was fulfilled in Him that day was this: "The Spirit of the Lord is upon Me because He hath anointed Me to preach the Gospel to

the poor" (Isa. 61: 1; Luke 4: 18). Some were quick
to perceive that a similar prophecy could be applied
to Him: "I will put My Spirit upon Him and He shall
show judgement to the Gentiles" (Isa. 42: 1; Matt.
12: 18). And to all this we may add His saying: "If
I cast out devils by the Spirit of God, then the Kingdom
of God is come unto you" (Matt. 12: 28). Truly the
Son of Man led a Spirit-filled life while He was here
on earth.

But the time had not then come for Him to fulfil
John the Baptist's promise and to baptize with the Holy
Ghost: "the Holy Ghost was not yet given because that
Jesus was not yet glorified" (John 7: 39). Elisabeth and
Zacharias had each been "filled with the Holy Ghost"
(Luke 1: 41,67); the Holy Ghost had "come" upon
Mary and "was" upon Simeon (Luke 1: 35; 2: 25).
But in each case, it was for one special purpose, and
there are no others except John the Baptist of whom
such a record exists in the Gospels. God Who gave the
Spirit without measure to His Son gave to no other
until His Son was glorified. He was the one truly Spirit-
filled man from the day of His own baptism until at
length the time came for Him to baptize with the Holy
Ghost. But He never lost sight of that divine object, and
it grew in His mind as His ministry moved to its close.
St. Luke records His words of promise and encourage-
ment as He entered on the last stage of that ministry:
"If ye then being evil know how to give good gifts unto
your children, how much more shall your heavenly
Father give the Holy Spirit to them that ask Him?"
(Luke 11: 13). St. John reveals how the Paraclete held

a dominant place in His thoughts on the eve of His death. Thus He told the Twelve what He had in view for them after He had gone from their midst: "I will pray the Father and He shall give you another Comforter that He may abide with you for ever" (John 14: 16). Then a little later He went on to explain: "When the Comforter is come . . . He shall testify of Me" (John 15: 26). And at last He made it clear that it would only be when He had returned to the Father that the heavenly Paraclete would come: "It is expedient for you that I go away: for if I go not away, the Comforter will not come unto you: but if I depart, I will send Him unto you" (John 16: 7). Thus the Holy Ghost is described as One "Whom the Father will send in My Name" (John 14: 26) and "Whom I will send unto you from the Father" (John 15: 26).

The next day He went to the Cross, and on the third morning He rose again. That night He came and stood in the midst of His friends as one who was soon to ascend to the right hand of God. They saw the print of the nails in His hands and they heard His word of peace and command. "And when He had said this, He breathed on them and saith unto them, Receive ye the Holy Ghost" (John 20: 22). These words describe a scene which was virtually sacramental in character, and there was a beautiful harmony between the outward and visible sign and the inward and spiritual grace. His action was remarkable and it receives dramatic emphasis from the nature of the word which St. John employed. It stands alone in the Gospel records; it was never used on any other occasion. But not only was the word never used; nowhere else do we

read of a kindred action. We are told how He touched
the eyes of the blind or the ears of the deaf with moisture
from His mouth, but we never read that He breathed
on any man apart from this special occasion. It was as
though He would convey the Holy Ghost to them by a
gift-deed to instruct and inspire their faith. A breath
of wind was a well-known emblem of the Spirit; the
same word in Greek means breath or wind or spirit.[1]
Thus there was an immediate kinship between the sign
which He employed and the words which He spoke:
"He BREATHED on them and saith unto them, Receive
ye THE HOLY BREATH". Did this mean that they were at
once endowed with the heavenly Paraclete? Comparison with other post-Resurrection sayings on this
subject is in favour of the view that it was symbolical.
The sign was prophetic in character; the words were
proleptic in intention. They would indeed receive the
Holy Ghost, but not until His exaltation was complete.
The sign and the saying anticipate what was yet to
take place.

There are very few post-Resurrection sayings about
the Holy Ghost in the Gospel records. St. Mark has
none at all; St. Matthew has only the one general
reference in the command to baptize "in the Name of
the Father and of the Son and of the Holy Ghost"
(Matt. 28: 19). St. Luke and St. John each have one
saying only, but they are both of the highest value. The
words in St. Luke are a match for the text in St. John
and form a guide to its proper meaning: "And behold,
I send the Promise of My Father upon you: but tarry
ye in the city of Jerusalem until ye be endued with
power from on high" (Luke 24: 49). There is no clear

note as to the time when the Lord said this, but the
textual evidence makes it reasonably clear that it was
after His appearance in Galilee and in or near Jerusalem. Thus He breathed on them and bade them
receive the Holy Breath on the evening of the day on
which He rose from the grave; and He pointed to the
Promise of His Father and told them to wait for it in
Jerusalem close to the time when He was to ascend.
St. John's saying belongs to the first and St. Luke's to
the last of the forty days in which He showed Himself
alive. The word PROMISE is used for the first time in the
Gospels in its technical character as "the promise of
God to His people" (cf. Acts 2 : 39), and it refers to the
Holy Spirit (cf. Isa. 44 : 3; Ezek. 36 : 27; Joel 2 : 28;
Zech. 12 : 10). Thus the PROMISE here means the thing
promised, and it fits the words in St. John: "I will pray
the Father, and He shall give you another Comforter"
(John 14 : 16). There is also a pronounced contrast
between the pronouns I and YE as He went on to stress
the need for patient waiting: it was for Him to send;
it was for them to wait until they had received and
were endued. Thus the Promise of the Father would be
fulfilled in their experience when they had been clothed
with power from on high; and both PROMISE and POWER
are linked with the Holy Spirit although His Name does
not occur.

The Acts connects itself with the Gospel after its
short preface by an indirect quotation of this passage:
"He . . . commanded them that they should not depart
from Jerusalem, but wait for the Promise of the Father"
(Acts 1 : 4). Then there is a sudden switch to direct
address, and St. Luke goes on to quote the Lord's own

saying: "Which, saith He, ye have heard of Me" (Acts 1: 4; cf. Luke 24: 49). Then the Promise of the Father is reinforced with a final reference to John's baptism: "For John truly baptized with water; but ye shall be baptized with the Holy Ghost not many days hence" (Acts 1: 5). This was the first occasion on which there was any reference to John's famous saying since it had been uttered shortly before the Lord had first appeared at the Jordan; and now it was taken up and endorsed by the risen Saviour with a decided emphasis. It was later quoted by Simon Peter and referred to by St. Paul (Acts 11: 16; 19: 4); but its immediate significance was made clear in the words of a yet more famous promise. This was voiced in reply to a question as they followed the path to the Mount of Olives just before His ascent: "Ye shall receive power when the Holy Ghost is come upon you" (Acts 1: 8 R.V.). The word for POWER in Greek provides the root from which English speech has derived such words as dynamo and dynamite.[2] This conveys the idea of tremendous force or explosive power. So we read of "Jesus of Nazareth, a man approved of God among you by miracles" (Acts 2: 22); "mighty works" (R.V.); "powers" (R.V.M.): and such "mighty works" were signs of the Messianic Kingdom, "the powers of the age to come" (Heb. 6: 5 R.V.). But this Greek noun has a cognate verb with a much softer meaning: "I am able".[3] Thus St. Paul used it in compound form in a fine passage: "I can do all things through Christ which STRENGTHENETH me" (Phil. 4: 13; cf. Eph. 6: 10). This may be paraphrased: "I am strong for all things in the strength of Him Who always MAKES ME ABLE." And the promise given just before

His ascent was in line with such use: "Ye shall receive POWER (something dynamic, something enabling), when the Holy Ghost is come upon you."

The "not many days hence" of which He had spoken were soon fulfilled; there were only ten days in all between the last scene on Olivet and the Feast of Pentecost. In an old book by W. Arthur, there is a fine passage on the value of those days of waiting: "Recall to mind that most wonderful silence of ten days—that long pause of the commissioned Church in sight of the perishing world. Never should the solemnity of that silence pass from the thoughts of any of God's people. It stands in the very forefront of our history—the Lord's most memorable and effective protest beforehand— that no authority under heaven, no training, no ordination could qualify men to propagate the Gospel without the baptism of the Holy Ghost."[4] The Lord Jesus had returned to heaven where He was to receive fresh "gifts for men" (Ps. 68 :18); the disciples on Olivet had returned to Jerusalem where they were to receive "power from on high" (Luke 24: 49). They had not been told when or how this would come to pass, but they would wait "with great joy" for the promised blessing (Luke 24: 52). St. Luke's Gospel says that they were "continually in the temple, praising and blessing God" (Luke 24: 53). The Acts says that they were continually in the house where they gave themselves "with one accord" to prayer and supplication (Acts 1: 14). Joy and expectation were interwoven with prayer and supplication throughout those ten days of earnest waiting. Thus "they were all with one accord

H

in one place" on the day of Pentecost when a startling
change swept through the whole house in which they
had gathered (Acts 2: 1). They heard the sound as of a
rushing mighty wind; they saw the sight as of a brightly
cloven flame: "and they were all filled with the Holy
Ghost and began to speak with other tongues as the
Spirit gave them utterance" (Acts 2: 4).

There was another occasion not long afterwards
when "the place was shaken where they were assembled
together and they were all filled with the Holy Ghost"
(Acts 4: 31). The rushing wind, the shaken house, and
the lambent flame were factors which all find an analogy in the experience of the prophet Elijah. When the
lonely Tishbite stood at the mouth of his cave at Horeb,
he was conscious of the mighty forces in the world of
nature before the Lord passed by. He heard the sound
of a rushing mighty wind that shook the valley with a
roar like crashing thunder; but the storm was to die
away, for the Lord was not in the wind. He felt the
force of a sudden heaving earthquake that rent the
rocks and made the mountains tremble; but the tremor
was to subside, for the Lord was not in the earthquake.
He saw the flames of a fiercely burning fire that swept
the valley and set the hills ablaze; but the blaze was to
pass away, for the Lord was not in the fire. Some yield
to the force of a gale; some are shaken by the terrors of
an earthquake; some are subdued by the devastating
realities of fire: but the prophet was not in need of
these, for he already had the qualities of all three in his
own character. They were allowed to die away because
they were no more than signs that the Lord was at
hand. He stood in need of a revelation from God, and

it came at last in "a still small voice" (1 Kings 19: 9.12). And so it was in the experience of the disciples on the day of Pentecost. They heard the sound as of a wind; they saw the sight as of a fire. But the Lord was not in the wind or fire; they were only signs that He was at hand. They passed away; then "they were all filled with the Holy Ghost".

The wind with its essential properties was a superb symbol of the Holy Spirit, and this came first in the experience of the disciples as in that of Elijah: "And suddenly there came a sound from heaven as of a rushing mighty wind: and it filled all the house where they were sitting" (Acts 2: 2). The Lord Himself had once referred to wind as an emblem of the Spirit's action: "The wind bloweth where it listeth and thou hearest the sound thereof, but canst not tell whence it cometh and whither it goeth: so is everyone that is born of the Spirit" (John 3: 8; cf. Ezek. 37: 9). The winds that blow where they list are like the Holy Spirit Who moves in the hearts of men as He wills. So the sound as of a rushing mighty wind bore down and filled the house where they sat. It was invisible; it was mysterious; they heard its sound, but did not feel its breath. It was not wind, but a sound AS OF wind; it was as though it swept through the house and shook it as the mountains had been shaken. The sound of that ghostly wind was the sign that the Lord was at hand. Samuel Taylor Coleridge has caught the same image in *The Rime of The Ancient Mariner* in which he describes a ship that lay in the grip of a calm as still as death. With loose and drooping sails, with scorched and shrinking decks, it was as idle as a painted ship upon a painted ocean. Men grew weak and listless until they spoke only to break the silence of the wide and breathless sea. Their cry went up from day to day: Let the wind blow! But one by one they died, and at last the desolate mariner was left to pace the deck alone. Then he began to pray, and soon there came the distant roar of ghostly wind. No breath of that strange wind ever reached the ship or fanned his cheek, but its sound shook the sails and drove it on to life and freedom. And the sound of the wind in the case of the Ancient Mariner was not unlike that sound AS OF wind which filled the house where they sat before they were filled with the Holy Ghost.

The fire with its essential properties was also a splendid symbol of the Holy Spirit, and this followed the wind in the experience of the disciples as in that of Elijah: "And there appeared unto them cloven tongues" ("tongues parting asunder", R.V.) "like as of fire, and it sat upon each of them" (Acts 2: 3). John the Baptist had once referred to fire as a symbol of the Spirit's presence: "He shall baptize you with the Holy Ghost and with fire" (Matt. 3: 11; cf. Exod. 3: 2). The fire that flashed from the bush in the experience of Moses is like the Holy Spirit Who burns in the hearts of men as He wills. So the sight as of a brightly glowing flame clave into tongues of fire which seemed to flicker like a candle over "each one of them" (R.V.). It was intangible; it was mysterious; they saw the flame, but did not feel its heat. The tongues were not fire, but LIKE AS OF fire; it was as though a sheet of flame had split into small jets of fire, and they in turn hovered over all who sat in the room. Archbishop Harrington

Lees has described a curious old Indian custom in the Yosemite Valley in the Sierra Nevada. The giant redwoods and the massive peaks which rise from the floor of the valley provide a setting of grandeur for the village and its people. Darkness is allowed to enfold the village at nightfall; then a fire is kindled on a ledge of rock three thousand feet above. At length a cry goes up from the valley: Let the fire fall! And the mountain watchman hears that cry in the still night air and sends a great cascade of fire hurtling over the cliff. It all tumbles over the edge into the dark void and descends to the valley below where the people light their fires from its blaze.[5] And that firefall in the Sierra Nevada is not unlike those tongues AS OF FIRE which came down on each of them before they were filled with the Holy Ghost.

Wind and fire are perhaps the least material of the natural elements which help to make a world that is material, and their very nature stamps them as the finest symbols of spiritual reality that nature affords. Thus the sound as of wind and the sight as of fire came with all the force of unearthly origin and dramatic energy. But the Lord was not in the wind nor in the fire; they were only signs that He was at hand. The noise and the stir were allowed to die away; then "they were all filled with the Holy Ghost" (Acts 2: 4). They were baptized with the Holy Ghost as John the Baptist had said (Matt. 3: 11); the Holy Ghost was now given because He was now glorified (John 7: 39). Peter declared that this was the basic factor in the experience in which they had thus shared: "Being by the right hand of God exalted and having received of the Father the promise of the Holy Ghost, He hath shed forth this which ye now see and hear" (Acts 2: 33). The wind and the fire were only passing phases in the history of those disciples, but the subsequent effusion of the Holy Spirit is a permanent principle and a vital necessity in the life of the Church. St. Luke records the historic precedent: THEY WERE FILLED (Acts 2: 4); St. Paul provides the apostolic command: BE YE FILLED (Eph. 5: 18). Our faith needs to ascend with this great *cri du coeur*: Let the wind of God blow! Let the fire of God fall!

"What a marvellous view there is from the summit of this mountain (The Mount of Olives)! To the west we were looking over the city of Jerusalem spread out below; to the east we could see the desolate wilderness reaching to the Dead Sea and the mountains of Moab. But it was neither west nor east that the Apostles were looking on that Ascension Day. They stood here gazing UP into heaven. And the early Church continued to do this, not literally, but spiritually. They were not looking back wistfully, cherishing the memory of a dead Christ. They were looking up in adoration and trustful obedience to the Risen, Ascended, Enthroned, Triumphant Lord, Who in due time would return in glory to complete His Kingdom. They knew that by His life and ministry, His passion and death, His resurrection and ascension, He had opened up the way into the presence of God, into heaven itself."

GODFREY ROBINSON AND STEPHEN WINWARD,
In the Holy Land, p. 120
Reproduced by kind permission of the Scripture Union

BIBLIOGRAPHY

C. J. ELLICOTT: *Historical Lectures on the Life of Our Lord Jesus Christ* (Sixth Edition) 1876

W. HANNA: *Our Lord's Life on Earth* 1882

H. C. G. MOULE: *Jesus and The Resurrection* (Fourth Edition) 1905

H. B. SWETE: *The Appearances of Our Lord after the Passion* 1915

A. PLUMMER: *The Gospel According to St. John* (Cambridge Greek Testament for Schools) 1882

B. F. WESTCOTT: *The Gospel According to St. John* (Eighteenth Impression) 1937

J. C. RYLE: *Expository Thoughts on the Gospel of St. Luke* (Popular Edition) 1896

J. C. RYLE: *Expository Thoughts on the Gospel of St. John* (Popular Edition) 1896

R. C. TRENCH: *Synonyms of the New Testament* (Eighth Edition) 1876

J. B. LIGHTFOOT: *Biblical Essays* 1893

NOTES

CHAPTER ONE

[1] H. C. G. Moule, p. 147.
[2] H. C. G. Moule, p. 147.
[3] B. F. Westcott, p. 300.
[4] B. F. Westcott, p. 300.
[5] H. C. G. Moule, p. 156.
[6] cf. C. J. Ellicott, p. 406, f.n. 1.
[7] H. C. G. Moule, p. 159.
[8] H. B. Swete, p. 56.
[9] W. Hanna, p. 620.
[10] H. C. G. Moule, p. 161.

CHAPTER TWO

[1] B. F. Westcott, p. 301.
[2] A. Plummer, p. 350.
[3] B. F. Westcott, p. 301.
[4] A. Plummer, p. 350.
[5] H. B. Swete, p. 58.
[6] A. Plummer, p. 350.
[7] H. C. G. Moule, p. 165.
[8] B. F. Westcott, p. 302.

CHAPTER THREE

[1] H. C. G. Moule, p. 174.
[2] B. F. Westcott, p. 303.
[3] ἀγαπάω; see R. C. Trench: *Synonyms of the New Testament*, p. 40.

[4] φιλέω; see R. C. Trench: *Synonyms of the New Testament*, p. 40.
[5] H. C. G. Moule, p. 180.
[6] H. B. Swete, p. 61.
[7] H. C. G. Moule, p. 188.
[8] ἀγαπᾶτε.

CHAPTER FOUR

[1] ἀγαπάω.
[2] φιλέω.
[3] cf. H. C. G. Moule, p. 181.
[4] B. F. Westcott, p. 303.
[5] A. Plummer, p. 353.
[6] H. C. G. Moule, pp. 185, 186.
[7] A. Chandler: *Ara Coeli*, p. 112.
[8] Charles Smyth: *The Friendship of Christ*, p. 10.
[9] G. G. Cragg: *Grimshaw of Haworth*, p. 62.
[10] Richard Baxter: *Practical Works*, Vol. XXIII, p. 419.

CHAPTER FIVE

[1] A. Plummer, p. 151.
[2] H. C. G. Moule, pp. 190–1.
[3] H. C. G. Moule, p. 193.
[4] B. F. Westcott, p. 304.
[5] δοξάσει.
[6] cf. H. C. G. Moule, p. 194.
[7] cf. B. F. Westcott, p. 304.
[8] cf. H. C. G. Moule, pp. 194–5.

CHAPTER SIX

[1] B. F. Westcott, p. 305.
[2] H. C. G. Moule, p. 202.
[3] H. B. Swete, p. 64.
[4] B. F. Westcott, p. 305.
[5] B. F. Westcott, p. 305.
[6] A. Plummer, pp. 355–6.
[7] cf. H. C. G. Moule, pp. 203–4.

CHAPTER SEVEN

[1] A. Plummer, p. 356.
[2] J. B. Lightfoot, p. 196.
[3] A. Plummer, p. 356.
[4] B. F. Westcott, p. 305.
[5] B. F. Westcott, p. 306.
[6] ὁ μαρτυρῶν.
[7] B. F. Westcott, p. 306.
[8] H. C. G. Moule, p. 198.
[9] A. Plummer, p. 356.
[10] A. Plummer, p. 357.
[11] J. B. Lightfoot, pp. 196-7; cf. also p. 196, fn. 2.
[12] A. Plummer, p. 357.
[13] This word is not in the Greek text.

CHAPTER EIGHT

[1] H. B. Swete, pp. 69-70.
[2] μαθητεύσατε: a Matthaean word (13: 52; 27: 57; 28: 19), but occurring also once in The Acts (14: 21) (cf. H. B. Swete, p. 73, fn.).
[3] Note the changes of tense: "The Lord thy God HATH BEEN with thee" (Deut. 2: 7); "IS with thee" (Joshua 1: 9); "WILL BE with thee" (2 Samuel. 14: 17).

4 Matt. 13: 39, 40, 49; 24: 3; 28: 20.
5 H. B. Swete, p. 81.
6 John Telford: *The Life of John Wesley*, p. 350.
7 F. W. Boreham: *A Bunch of Everlastings, or Texts That Made History*, pp. 131–3.

CHAPTER NINE

1 H. B. Swete, pp. 102–3.
2 The Walk to Emmaus was quite different in character.
3 J. C. Ryle: *Expository Thoughts on St. Luke*, Vol. 11, p. 525.
4 Alfred Lord Tennyson: *The Passing of Arthur* (lines 460, 461).

CHAPTER TEN

1 H. B. Swete, p. 106.
2 H. B. Swete, p. 149.
3 F. F. Bruce: *Commentary on The Book of The Acts*, p. 41.

EPILOGUE

1 πνεῦμα.
2 δύναμις.
3 δύναμαι.
4 W. Arthur: *The Tongue of Fire*, p. 192.
5 Archbishop Harrington Lees, in the opening address at the Constitutional Convention in Sydney, 1926.